REAL ESTATE INVESTING IN YOUR 20'S

Your Rise to Real Estate Royalty

Ross Hamilton

authorHOUSE®

AuthorHouse™
1663 Liberty Drive
Bloomington, IN 47403
www.authorhouse.com
Phone: 1-800-839-8640

First published by AuthorHouse 12/10/2009

ISBN: 978-1-4490-5813-5 (e)
ISBN: 978-1-4490-5812-8 (sc)

Printed in the United States of America
Bloomington, Indiana

This book is printed on acid-free paper.

"The main reason I decided to dedicate myself to real estate is because I have a burning desire not to be a slave to money. A nine-to-five job with one week of vacation is my definition of jail. Having a roof over my head on how much I can make would drown my spirits. Basing my retirement on someone else's company policy or hoping there will still be social security is a gamble I am not willing to take. Having the government tax me before I get paid and then tax me on everything I buy is unnecessary. Not being able to pass a decent legacy to my children would be childish. Not being able to teach my children how to enjoy life by having their money work for them would be embarrassing, and having my boss ask me, "Ross, do you want Thanksgiving or Christmas off this year?" is out of the question and sounds like a loose form of slavery to me."

Table ofContents

Acknowledgments:

My thanks goes to my mother and father who have always believed in me; to Taylor, my wife who has always stood by me, and the loving memory of my grandmother Ruth Hamilton, who's memories will always put a smile on my face. Thank you all for providing the fuel that drives me.

A special thanks to my many mentors whose teachings have had a profound impact on me.

And to all of you who know they have the ability to rise to royalty.

Featured on MSNBC's website:

Real Estate Entrepreneur Creates Invitation-Only Social Network for Fellow Investors Amidst 'Historic Opportunities'

SAN FRANCISCO – Social networks and the whole interactive Web 2.0 phenomenon have been a dominant feature of social life and the news media lately, and millions regularly spend countless hours each month on sites like Facebook, Twitter, and Linked-In. One startup company with a more selective vision for a real estate investor oriented social network decided to focus on the quality of members as opposed to quantity.

The invitation-only community, Connected Investors.com (http://www.ConnectedInvestors.com Use promo code 'Ross'), was founded in 2005 by real estate investor, entrepreneur, and author, Ross Hamilton. Hamilton says he started the real estate investor focused social network to help other investors create a community to support each other as well as to serve as an online way to track deal flow and utilize all of the best-of-breed available web marketing tools like automated customer list building, automatic customer follow up, and audio/video compatibility,

Hamilton, author of "**Real Estate Investing in your 20s**," also indicated that part of his motivation was to build a personal network because, "it was a little lonely working as a full-time real estate investor in my 20s. I didn't have many peers my age, so I just focused on networking with other investors."

"We at Connected Investors believe that now is a historic time in real estate and that sophisticated real estate investors who have access to the best tools and technology will be able to create wealth for their families and help America come out of the worst housing crisis since the Great Depression," continued Hamilton.

Showing that the members of Hamilton's social network are in smart company, Sequoia Equities (http://www.experiencesequoia.com) today highlighted the launch of a distressed real estate platform called Sequoia Debt Ventures (SDV). With institutional players like Sequoia Equities (who currently manage $1.6 billion worth of real estate) focusing on buying residential real estate from banks, lenders, private equity firms, and other investors, individual investors may very well need to create their own networks to level the playing field.

Hamilton emphasized his website and network is designed to, "show investors how to use the Internet to make more money in their real estate business right now."

About the Author

Fans of ESPN's X-Games may have seen Ross Hamilton gracing the front cover of BMX freestyle magazines. Readers of MSNBC may have seen Ross hailed as an entrepreneur whose company has grown over 400% during "tough" economic times. Either way, Ross' "No pain no gain" attitude fuels each page of this amazing book. Believing that starting out with nothing makes it easy to risk everything, Ross moved over ten million dollars worth of real estate in his first 3 years of investing.

In addition to his real estate accomplishments, Ross is an author, speaker, educator and the sole founder of ConnectedInvestors.com. The depth of his experience has enabled him to further contribute to the real estate success of others by serving as a boardmember for a prominent real estate investment association. Ross is known for challenging the "traditional" educational path to success. He takes great pride in providing the people of his generation financial hope and direction during a time of uncertainty.

Ross wrote this book to serve as a compass to guide your rise to real estate royalty, *Real Estate Investing in Your 20's* provides young, motivated investors with solid directions and proven instructions that if followed will lead to success. When you finish reading this amazing story, you will know how to: Get a free hands-on education worth thousands, receive over a 100% ROI (Return on investment) when investing your own cash, and where to find the resources you will need. This book is designed to speed up your learning curve 1000%.

While you are turning the pages of this book, your heart rate will rise as you feel excitement, peril and anticipation for huge profits. Real Estate Investing In Your 20's covers important topics most books ignore such as: Religion in real estate, why you should never work with young professionals, hanging with the super rich, why the secret service would want to get involved, the local mafia, the importance of family, and much more.

If you want to rise to royalty with real estate, you better be ready for it all. This book will equip you with the knowledge and direction necessary to claim your real estate kingdom. To ensure your success, the author has also included a bonus worth over $1740.00 located in this book.

Introduction

To help you make money in real estate, it is important that you understand why I have spent the last seven years of my life writing this book. You may or may not know this, but most popular real estate books are not written by the name on the cover. Most real estate books are slapped together in about three weeks. This book is different. It is not a reflection on my *past* experiences—rather, it was written *during* my experiences. Writing this book while I was taking my journey to financial independence, I have ended up with a very unique valuable record I want to share with you because I believe it is important for you to get the truth about real estate investing.

This book gives you a look through my eyes during each critical step of the journey. I have carefully written and reviewed every chapter of this book.

The day you make the decision to become a real estate investor will change your life. "When a caterpillar turns into a butterfly, does it know how beautiful it has become?" Becoming an investor is like coming out of the cocoon of the traditional life mold, and turning into a modern-day monetary iconoclast. It is vital that people get involved in real estate investing at as young an age as possible.

Don't let anyone fool you: It will take you some time to start seeing money. At first you must dedicate a lot of time and energy to building systems. It's easier to dedicate the amount of time necessary for the startup of a real estate business when you're young because you don't have a family to support on top of everything else. Instead of going to a PTA meeting, you can go to an REIA meeting. Instead of reviewing your child's homework, you can review your marketing plan. Instead of having to pay big bucks every month for a family health insurance plan, you can spend that money on advertising.

Dedicate yourself to real estate today, and you will not have to choose between family or work in the future. I cannot advocate strongly enough the importance of getting involved in real estate when you are young. I would like you to do a little experiment: Find someone who is about double your age. Ask him or her this question: "If you had bought one house a year every year from the time you were my age until the present day, what do you think would be different about your life?" This person will give you all the reasons why you need to start investing today.

Chapter 1—The Early Mindset of a Millionaire

"To know the road ahead, ask someone coming back."—
Chinese proverb

Money is what makes someone royalty in the modern day. Once upon a time, it was kings and queens; now it's millionaires and billionaires—in other words, pure power. Most people dream of being a millionaire and once awakened, accept being a millionaire as just a dream. I know the art of acquiring money starts in the mind. At 20 years old, I know I would wear my crown in the near future.

My original plan was to fall into the rat race by starting my young adult life off in debt through college loans, begging someone for a job in a field I didn't go to school for and purchasing depreciating assets on credit to bring temporary relief to my situation. Like most, I looked at true wealth as an exclusive club I was not invited to. The members of this club consisted mainly of individuals who were born rich. In my mind the rich had a monopoly over money. This mindset changed when I finally decided to open my eyes and take control.

"You cannot win a game of Monopoly©
without real estate"
Ross Hamilton

When you were younger, did you wish to be a skilled warrior? Maybe you wanted to be a samurai or a medieval knight. Even if you didn't run around your house chasing your younger brother with a wrapping paper tube pretending to be a knight like I did, I'm sure you were witness to children imitating ancient warriors. When you were young, they were so cool. They had the skills, the weapons, the clothing—and they always got the girl.

If you're reading this book, you have more in common with samurai warriors than you might think. Medieval knights and samurai warriors were ancient real estate investors. Huh? It's true; these warriors risked it all to get paid in land. Acquiring large amounts of land was their main motivation. If a samurai won enough battles, he would have enough land to "employ" other samurai to fight for him. Whoever had more land was king.

This book is subtitled *Rise to Royalty* because we are going to give you the modern-day skills to quickly fight your way to the throne.

Now that you realize you're a modern-day samurai, everything just got a lot more exciting. Throughout history, the main difference between wealthy people and poor people has been the amount of property they own. If history repeats itself as it often does, and the world lasts long enough, maybe one day kids will put on a suit, grab a contract and a business card, and pretend to be a real estate investor.

If you are ready to put some fire under your ass, rally up everyone you know, pull together all of your resources, and rise to royalty— you are reading this book for the right reason. Get ready for the ride of a lifetime!

Chapter 2—Why Real Estate?

"The beginning is the most important part of the work."
—Plato

Before you read any further, I want to make it very clear that if you wish to multiply your chances for success, you need a strong reason *why* you want to succeed. This will be the fuel to keep your inner desire burning. This chapter will explain why you should consider spending a lot of your efforts building a real estate portfolio; however, for all of this to work, you need to tell real estate why *it* should invest in *you*.

Real estate has everything you could ever want or dream about. You could become a celebrity like Donald Trump, or live a wealthy, quiet life with all the time in the world for family and friends. Why do you want to succeed in real estate? The answer to that question must provide motivation through some financially and personal trying times.

This book will show how a 22-year-old "C" student went from having less than $38 dollars in the bank to $380,000 in net worth in less than 20 months (a 10,000 percent gain). The reason *why* is what kept my sights on the goal and success clear in my mind. When you are trying to achieve something and have a strong reason behind your goal, people will sense your passion and typically will not stand in your way. You already have your reason why. Identify the abstract and use it.

Real estate investing made sense to me because I realized that in any logical decision-making, it is more common to succeed if you play the odds. Imagine this: I give you magic dice; you examine the dice and notice four sides are blue and the other two sides are red. I explain that all you have to do is roll the dice—and if you guess what color the dice land on, you will have instant financial freedom. Before you roll one of the die I say, "Go ahead and bet, red or blue!" Unless you just did not want to win, is there any reason why you would bet against the odds?

I used this same logic in determining what business I wanted to study. I found more millionaires are made in real estate than any other business. In fact, 80 percent of self-made millionaires achieve their wealth through real estate. What that means is, if you want to be a millionaire and you plan on doing so through any business other than real estate, the odds are stacked against you. Start off in a business that favors success.

In real estate, your product is almost always going up in value and you are able to take advantage of the best tax benefits. My favorite aspect of real estate is the fact you can leverage $10,000 into $100,000 and $100,000 into $1,000,000.

The main reason I decided to dedicate myself to real estate is because I have a burning desire not to be a slave to money. A nine-to-five job with one week of vacation is my definition of jail. Having a roof over my head on how much I can make would drown my spirits. Basing my retirement on someone else's company policy or hoping there will still be social security is a gamble I am not willing to take. Having the government tax me before I get paid and then tax me on everything I buy is unnecessary. Not being able to pass a decent legacy to my children would be childish. Not being able to teach my children how to enjoy life by having their money work for them would be embarrassing, and having my boss ask me, "Ross, do you want Thanksgiving or Christmas off this year?" is out of the question and sounds like a loose form of slavery to me.

Those are some of my reasons why. All you need is a reason that will motivate you. Once your portfolio is built, it will make you money for the rest of your life. Being young, you have plenty of time for appreciation and compounded interest.

Perhaps you've pondered the question, "What is the most powerful force in the universe?" Albert Einstein pondered this same question. Let's take a look at a direct quote from Albert: "The most powerful force in the universe is compounded interest." The logic behind this answer should excite you if you are a young investor, because you can put the most powerful force in the universe to work on your portfolio today.

Let's take a quick look at the reason why—regardless of your age—you need to start getting the most powerful force in the universe working for you today. Say you're 24 years old and your goal is to have more than $1 million in cash by the time you are 65. Seems like a tall order; however, with the power of compounded interest you will only have to put away $2,000 a year for six years at 12 percent interest. By the time you're 65, your portfolio will be worth exactly $1,074,968. Or let's say you waited until you were 30 to start taking advantage of compounded interest. You decided instead of investing your money, you wanted to buy a nice car. You would have to invest $2,000 a year for 27 years at 12 percent to reach a similar goal by age 65. That is a $54,000 investment instead of $12,000 because you waited six years to use the most powerful force in the universe.

Still, to invest $54,000 and end up with a million is a very good deal. So if you're in your thirties, by all means the time is now. If you are in your early twenties, do whatever you can to pull together funds to invest.

In this book, however, we are not going to be talking about making 12 percent on your money. Compounded interest, although powerful, is too slow to keep most people's attention. If you're not excited about investing, then it's just a job, and our goal is not to create another job. It's to turn real estate investing into a very profitable hobby. Hobbies are something you look forward to doing on the weekends. You will stay up late at night and get up early in the morning because they are fun for you.

How can we turn up the juice on compounded interest and get you excited about investing money rather than spending it? What if instead of making 12 percent on your money you made 250 percent? Would you be excited about investing $5,000 if it was going to bring you back $12,500? Then you invest the $12,500 and bring back $31,500! Would you stay up late at night and work on the weekends? If you were looking at a car, would you temporarily settle for the less expensive car and put the rest of your funds toward the 250 percent investment, wait a couple of years, and buy the car of your dreams—with cash? These are rhetorical questions because I assume that if you are reading this book you are either academically smart and want to explore how to set up a safe financial future, or you are street smart and want to apply your hustle to something that could bring you wealth.

So now that we have all agreed a 250 percent return on investment (ROI) would be great, how can we achieve such a return with every investment? This may seem like a tall order. Prior to diving into the answer, let me ask you one more question, how much can you lift? Let's say you can lift 100 pounds. Now, how much could you lift/make with the proper leverage? Answer: any amount you desire. In this book I am going to describe the discipline and knowledge necessary to leverage the most powerful force in the universe.

I typically see over a 250 percent return on my cash when I invest it in real estate. Receiving 250 percent on your money will turn you into a millionaire very fast. Your friends will typically be confused and slightly envious, the opposite sex will be attracted, and your family will be either worried or impressed. When your girlfriend's/ boyfriend's parents find out you own several properties, they will love you. Your friends are flipping burgers and you are flipping houses. What do you think that will do to your confidence?

Once your confidence is on the rise, you will attract more successful people into your sphere of influence, and not only will that bring with it an infinite number of opportunities, but you will realize you can honestly take your life in whatever direction you choose. Once you are out of the rat race, you can't help but build business around the things you enjoy. Now you are involved in businesses that are fun, and this makes you a more successful person because you enjoy life.

Looking back: *This book reads as if you are looking through my eyes while I was on my rise to real estate royalty. These "looking back" items were written years after each section was originally put together and will provide you with quick but important information on a particular situation.*

Research: *I will designate specific topics of outside research that will be vital to your real estate success. If you are an investor you will never be able to stop learning. Make sure to document the research I assign.*

Homework: *I will assign you simple homework assignments you must do to reach your goals.*

WARNING: Although I moved over ten million dollars of real estate in my first few years of investing and have done nothing but live real estate for the last 8 years of my life, most of you will come up with a reason not to follow my advice. To be exact, over 80% of you will not complete one homework or research assignment.

This book is an easy read because 90% of the learning will come from your homework and research assignments. If you choose not to take the proactive steps necessary you WILL fail.

Failing in real estate means; losing a ton of money, foreclosure, bankruptcy, and all of the issues that go along with having no money. These words have been designed to scare you. This business is no joke. I have never lost money on a real estate investment because I continue to educate myself. Real estate can make or break your life.

The homework and research assignments are not an option. Prior to getting into the next chapter, answer the following questions:

1.   Do you want to be successful?

2.   Are you the type of person who takes action?

3.   Do you often follow through with your goals?

4.   Will you complete at least 1 homework and research assignment?

Chapter 3—Starting Off With Nothing at All

"Starting off with nothing makes it easy to risk everything."

August 17, 2004

I'm 22 years old, and I have earned my associate's degree in business management. I now have a lot of free time on my hands. I have decided to spend a lot of that time at Barnes and Noble reading books on how to acquire money. I have been studying real estate, stocks, psychology, negotiation, networking, and anything I could use as a tool to acquire power. I've never had the patience to sit down and read a book of fiction, but give me a book on real estate, and I would finish it as fast as I could. What really helped me was to summarize a book in my own words. I would take a 300-page book and recap it into six information-packed pages. This was great because I could quickly brush up on negotiation, selling, and psychology right before I needed to apply the skill.

I currently live in Wilmington, North Carolina. This area has had an amazing amount of real estate growth, and everyone speculates on the potential for steady growth for years to come. I saw the quickest path to royalty in real estate. So I decided to stop talking about it and put my money where my mouth is.

I quit my job and decided to claim my crown.

I signed up to take the class to get my real estate license. Even if you don't want to hold a broker's license, it is a good idea to take your local real estate class. You need to understand all the vocabulary 100 percent so you can convince clients, private investors, and other agents you know what you're talking about. It is also very important to understand real estate laws, HUD statements, and contracts.

A short time after completing the real estate class, I was reading the newspaper looking for information on the meeting of my local Real Estate Investment Association (REIA). One book I'd read emphasized how important it was to be a member of your local investors' meeting. There was a seminar coming up titled *Secrets of Local Real Estate Investors*. I attended the seminar and listened to what the three investors had to say. I noticed that only one of them, John, seemed to be successful. After the seminar I wanted to speak specifically to John. I almost chickened out, but then I remembered a quote from the networking book I had been brushing up on right before I entered the seminar room:

> *"Knowledge without application is like having no knowledge at all."—Bob Burg, Endless Referrals*

I didn't study for months to walk out of that seminar without applying some of my knowledge. I took a deep breath and pushed my way through the crowd of people standing around John. Thoughts were whirling around in my mind…. It was going to cost me close to $1,000 to activate my real estate license. I'd been saving for years and had about $5,500 in the bank. I just had to ask a pro his opinion about the necessity of having a real estate license.

I interrupted John's conversation and asked, "Just starting out, should I get my real estate license so I can become familiar with buying and selling houses?"

After the laughter faded from the group of older investors standing in a circle, John answered, "Do you want to show kitchens or make money?"

Obviously, I replied, "I want to make money."

He told me to buy options on houses and wholesale them to people at the REIA meeting. During his talk at the seminar, he had said he didn't want to tell us all his secrets, but there was so much business in town he couldn't do all the deals himself. I asked John if I could help him in any way, and he gave me his card and told me to call him. To say the least, I was very excited to have an opportunity to work with a successful real estate investor.

I went home and immediately reviewed my notes on how to successfully follow up with business contacts. I took a head shot of myself and incorporated it into an e-mail to John, thanking him for his time and letting him know I would be in touch with him in the near future. I felt as if I had just scored a cheerleader's phone number, and I was trying to figure out how long I should wait to call. Do I play it cool, or show interest and bring flowers? I'd met John on a Thursday, sent him e-mail on Friday, and decided to call him the following Tuesday. Here's how the conversation went:

"Hi, John, this is Ross Hamilton. We met at the seminar Thursday. Do you have a minute to talk?"

"Yeah, I have a minute."

"I'm really interested in everything you have going on and was wondering if you could use me at the moment?"

"Are you in school?"

"I just graduated with a business management degree, and I've finished the North Carolina real estate class."

"You know what, Ross; I'm going to do something with you. I'll put you on a referral list; basically, you refer me business and I give you $500. Most people do two a week.

Well, you could make more than that, actually. Why don't we just meet for lunch and we will go over everything?"

"Sounds great."

That's where I'm at right now. Tomorrow I'm meeting with John for lunch, and I will see if his offer is as good as it sounds. The main thing I am trying to gain from this guy is his how-to and his contacts. All my life my dad told me, "Whatever business you want to own, work for your competition first. Find out how they operate, get all of their contacts, and start your own business learning from your boss' mistakes."

This is my chance. John is the top investor in southeastern North Carolina. Even if he gives me a crappy job and I'm not making any money, I will put up with it—as long as I can learn his tactics and start applying what I have been researching for so long.

I believed this contact was going to be worth its weight in gold to me.

The best advice I have for you right now is to go to as many seminars as possible, build up a list of professionals, read as many books as you can, and remember that "knowledge without application is like having no knowledge at all."

Looking back: *Your net worth is almost always determined by your network. You have to network to be successful in any area of life—especially real estate. If you want to make it you cannot be shy. You cannot be afraid to ask questions. Your success will often be determined by how many uncomfortable situations you put yourself into. Get uncomfortable and watch the success roll in.*

Should you quit your job and focus all your efforts on real estate investing like I did? Only you have the answer to that question. You can accomplish a lot as an investor while having a full time job. Most investors have other jobs. However, "Burning the ship" will force you to make things happen.

Homework: *Find and attend the closest REIA. (Real Estate Investment Association.) Collect at least 5 business cards.*

Extra credit: *Take the class to become a real estate agent. You do not have to activate your license, however you need to really study the ins and outs of this business.*

Note* If you choose not to do your homework, no one is going to send your parents a report card with a failing grade. You will just fail in your mission to make money in real estate.

Chapter 4—Opportunity

"Someone once told me: 'Luck is when opportunity meets preparation.'"

August 20, 2004

Finally! The opportunity I've been looking for! I met with John for lunch and things went great. He is giving me a chance, which is all I wanted. I feel he is testing me. My job description is to find properties that look like they need to be sold. What I am most excited about is the opportunity to ask a successful investor his opinion on investment opportunities. I know this will speed up my learning curve by 1,000 percent. Even though I feel this is a job Mr. Long would give a monkey, I will do the best job I can to show him I take this opportunity very seriously. If I am able to find John profitable investments, I know I will be able to take on more responsibility. This will allow me to oversee many investments and learn by trial and error. I know this will help me build up an important quality I lack right now because I am so wet behind the ears: confidence. I have the determination to rise to royalty, but my confidence will have to be fueled by education and experience.

It's time for me to prove myself. John has given me an opportunity to work with him and I will not fail. I've devised a plan to find more properties than John can handle. My brother delivers pizza, my good friend is a meter reader, and I am close with people in many different trades through my father's business. I've already sat down with many of my friends and relatives and showed them examples of the type of house I'm looking for. I offered them $10 every time they bring me a photo and address, and $100 every time John purchases a property. Within the first week, my contacts brought me a lot of properties to look at. I soon learned that the hard part was not finding potential investments. The hard part was getting the owner of the home on the phone.

September 27, 2004

After one month of monkeying around working all day every day to find a house that looks like it needs to be bought, finding the owner, and setting up an appointment with John, I have not received one paycheck. In fact, the last month actually cost me money for 16 photos plus my car expenses. Since I am not in the habit of wasting my time, I set up an appointment with John to get his advice on finding homes.

As I was discussing my plan to find suitable properties with John, he had to take a phone call in another office. While he was out of the room I felt this was an opportunity to pull a "James Bond." I quickly looked through some of his files. I was determined to find out where he was getting most his leads. I was going broke and failing was not an option. As I was riffling through his files I noticed in each files there was a "Seller worksheet." I quickly examined each of these worksheets and noticed there was a lot of information on the homeowner's bank account. I put all of his files back and quickly sat back down. When John came back into the room, I asked him if it would be important for me to find the homeowner's bank information as well as the other info I had been gathering on each property. He said that would be necessary only if they were behind on their payments. After a couple more questions, it was apparent to me he was receiving most of his revenue through pre-foreclosures.

The next day I decided to be proactive and make a trip to the local courthouse. I figured I might be able to bring John some useful information. I copied down all the information posted on the foreclosure board. There were two other people there, taking down the same information. Later, I sat down with John and showed him the information, hoping he would be pleasantly surprised.

John responded: "I have someone taking care of that for me; keep looking for properties around town."

Not to be ungrateful—because just two months ago I thought this guy was worth his weight in gold—but I was getting frustrated. I had been driving around for months. Out of 10 houses I usually found two owners. When I set up an appointment for them to meet with John, they didn't want to sell for the price we would offer! I had only found one deal in the prior two months: $500 for two months of work. I could make more sitting on the corner with a sign. Many of my friends were working normal jobs making $500 to $700 a week, and I couldn't even go out with them because I was not making any money.

I was sitting on my front porch looking at my diminishing finances. I noticed a jogger run by. This guy was soaked in sweat; he was putting everything he had into it just to stay moving, and he wasn't even moving very fast. About 30 seconds later I watched a couple of people on bikes fly by, and my frustration was taken over by a smile. I realized that

jogging is like having a normal job; if you want to get anywhere you have to work hard. Real estate is like riding a bike; you can push real hard and coast for a while. Better yet, once set up correctly you can coast forever.

Right then I was learning how to put my "bike" together. Even though my friends were moving, once my 10-speed bike was together, I would easily catch up with them and coast right by—even if they were 100 miles ahead.

This thought sparked my second wind of motivation. I printed out a picture of someone putting together a bike and put it in my wallet.

How could I become part of the pre-foreclosure business? I needed answers, so I did what I always did and went to Barnes and Noble and found a real estate book with the most information on short sales. I didn't buy it because I could not afford it. The book was $24.99. But I did read the entire book and made a summary on short sales. What I realized is, if you are buying properties of any sort, and don't know how to do a short sale, you will miss out on a lot of opportunities. I strongly recommend you educate yourself on short sales. *(The simple definition of a short sale is when a bank sells a property for less than they are owed, for example, if the bank wrote a mortgage for $100,000 on a property and sold it for $80,000.)*

After mulling over the process on how you market to properties that you may be able to short sale, I had a good marketing idea. Every book basically tells you to go to the courthouse, gather names of people behind on their mortgage, and send them letters. But I had to find a way to separate John's company from the other companies that were soliciting short-sale properties.

My simple plan was to put together an audio CD that explained how John's company could help. I would be a student interviewing John and asking him the questions that someone behind on their payments might have about the foreclosure process. We would include this CD with our letter, which would instantly set us apart. This would also serve as a first hand learning experience for me.

I presented my idea to John, and he gave it the green light. He told me every time we got a deal because of my CD, he would compensate me for it. This was step one toward getting in on the pre-foreclosure business.

Looking back: *At the time I did not realize how important it was for me to find someone to work with. This one move wound up propelling me toward financial independence at an amazingly fast rate. John and I ultimately did hundreds of deals together, and I was able to not only learn what to do, but more importantly learn what not to do. We made millions together—though we also lost a huge amount of money, I was learning on someone else's dollar.*

Research: *Short sales.*

Homework: *Call each of the five investors you met at your local REIA and ask them if you can take them out to lunch. Once you get the chance to sit down with an investor, simply ask each investor how you can help them make money.*

Chapter 5—The First Property

"Going to your first real estate closing is like getting married."

November 3, 2004

The biggest move of my investing career is unfolding. At 22 years of age, I'm buying my first house. I have talked about it for over three years, and after being presented a decent opportunity, I decided to put up or shut up. This is the deal: The house is worth $140,000; an investor purchased for $60,000 and put $20,000 into the rehab. The investor has $80,000 invested, and after some negotiation has agreed to sell it to me for $109,000. This price includes his paying all closing costs, so there is no money out of my pocket. What makes the deal even sweeter is that he has a tenant going into the house paying $875 a month, with a two-year option to purchase at $130,000.

The only problem is that I still have way less than $10,000 in the bank and no real job. So I am pulling out all the stops, putting into action all the ideas I've been storing in my notebook about how to get around being a broke college kid—whenever the right opportunity presented itself.

The other issue I've run into is getting a decent rate on 100 percent financing for an investment property. I will have to come up with something creative to get around this red tape. Fortunately, I had great credit getting into all this. If you are planning on getting traditional financing, you will need to see where your credit stands ASAP.

I was so tired of talking about being a real estate investor that nothing was going to stop me from purchasing this house. Although the investment was not exactly a home run—it was only going to net me a cash flow of about $50 per month—it would help me build good credit. What I was most excited about was that the tenant would be paying down my mortgage as the property value continued to rise. As long as I could keep this property afloat, there was no reason I wouldn't get a very nice check one day. I could also take out an equity line to help me purchase more properties. Once I closed on this house, my "bike" would be ready to ride.

Having Doubts
November 29, 2004

My loan was closing in two days and I was starting to have doubts. This was a 30-year commitment. No matter what happened to this property, I would have to deal with it. Going to your first closing is like getting married. Signing the papers is taking a legal vow. I was looking through the closing documents and one of the first bold statements reads: *To **have and to hold** the property, to trustee, its successors and assigns, but upon the trust, and under the terms and conditions of this Deed of Trust, to which Grantor, Trustee and Beneficiary hereby agree.* This means you are bound together through the good times (cash flow) and the bad (expensive repairs/ vacancies.)

This was going to be my property and my responsibility to keep it up and running. Signing the papers meant I couldn't take off for months at a time, or do any of those things you say you're going to do once you're out of college. The day before closing I drove by the property and stared at it for about an hour. If I ever wanted to be financially free, I had to take some risks. I took a deep breath and thought of all the rentals I'd been in…the carefree way of living, just using a house and moving on, not worrying about repairs or values.

After I realized I was here for bigger things than just moving in and out of rental homes, my hesitation turned into excitement and I closed on the deal.

Looking back: *This was not a great deal and I would never do a deal like this today. Many people get anxious to buy their first property and purchase a home that might not be the best deal. Although I made over $30,000.00 on this deal when I finally closed it, it was a problem property for me for a long time. Once taxes were reassessed in my area I was going negative $200.00 a month on the property for about two years. The real cash flow will always be less than you first anticipate. Looking back on closing this deal I am really surprised I was actually able to get a loan. I had no real job, no experience, and no real clue what I was doing, and the bank just gave me 100 percent of the money I needed. From my standpoint, I had nothing to lose. I had none of my own money in this deal! What other business can someone just decide they want to get into, no matter how completely oblivious they may be and receive, in my case, $100,000 to give it a try?*

Research:
Lease Options
How to improve your credit

Chapter 6—You've Got to Work on Yourself

"The richest man is the one with the most powerful friends."—Altobello to Vincent, *Godfather 3*

The Mentor
December 17, 2004

You must find a real estate mentor to help speed up your learning curve. The last two homework assignments I gave you had to do with finding a mentor. Right now, put this book down and find a mentor. There is nothing you could do that would help your success more. The great thing about finding a mentor is that it's really not that hard. There is not one investor who would turn away a motivated individual who wants to work on commission. Look in the paper for all the "We buy houses" ads and go to your REIA meeting. The great thing about being young is that the investors you speak with will not feel threatened by you. Make sure you find an experienced mentor who has access to a lot of money. Once you have a pipeline of deals coming in, you want to make sure you can capitalize on all of them. When you meet with your mentor, find out if he or she has any real estate courses you can review. My mentor has about 10 courses and is always looking for education on something he doesn't know about.

Although I am an apprentice, I know I will be a mentor one day. In this business, if you want to make it big you need a good referral network and a lot of trained eyes out there looking for opportunities. People like you and me will not let anything stand in the way on our climb to success. My philosophy is to help as many people as I can rise to royalty so I can have powerful friends who will be more than happy to help me.

There is a certain level of trust you must have in your mentor. At the end of the day, if you do a deal with your mentor and he or she decides not to pay you, it would be expensive for you to enforce whatever pay arrangement you have made. In many cases, mentors will give you a percentage of the profit. To find out how fair your mentor is going to, use this rule of thumb: If you and a mentor go out to lunch for a meeting and he or she pays, take notice of your server. If he or she does a good job refilling drinks, there are no mess-ups, and the waitress makes the normal small talk after the bill is paid, take notice of the tip left. Ninety-nine percent of the time this will be a great indication of how the mentor will treat you.

Make an Easy Million?
December 22, 2004

For everyone who has seen the infomercials and book titles about how easy it is to make millions in real estate, this section is for you. Those titles and concepts are a great way to sell books, but that's about it. (Those types of books should be in the fiction section!) Take notice, there is nothing in the title of this book about making millions. No one is going to hand you hundreds of thousands of dollars. As a matter of fact, most people will try to take opportunities away from you. You have to be creative and learn how to deal with many different types of people. Every book I've read on real estate gives you a step-by-step plan on how to become a millionaire. It is a beautiful thought, and before I started, I believed it would be easy money.

The idea of anyone being able to coach you through real estate reminds me of when I taught BMX freestyle lessons. I could never fully prepare students to deal with everything they would encounter once they hit a ramp and took flight. There are a million different ways to do the same trick. As long as you land on two wheels, you are a success. I would show or explain to my students how I would approach a certain stunt; however, most of my success in teaching came from providing confidence and motivation. Seeing makes believers. Once my students watched me enough times and had it in their heads they could do it, my job was done.

When I first started riding BMX, I was lucky enough to ride with Dave Mirra. Dave was (Still is) the world's best BMX rider. I got good fast because of the talent I surrounded myself with.

If you want real estate investing to be your main source of income, you are going to have to surround yourself with talent, give it 100 percent and be ready to pay your dues. This business is not a secret; however, only the people with a strong reason *why* actually rise to royalty and live the dream. My mentor, John, told me the only reason he keeps me around is because of my persistence. "Until you know what you are doing, the only thing you have to offer is your hustle." – Don Hamilton

> ***Looking back:*** *You must understand that if you have no real estate knowledge, no contacts, and no money, it will take time to rise to royalty. At first don't measure your success in dollars, because as long as you're persistent the money will come. Instead measure your initial success by how much knowledge you obtain, contacts you make, and money to which you gain access to.*

Self-Control
January 15, 2005

This will be the make-or-break section for many investors in their twenties. If you cannot control your schedule, partying, and sex drive, you will have a very hard time being successful in real estate. Successful people are able to control the outside influences that will cloud their goals. I looked at my life and realized most of my motivation came from the desire for the opposite sex. If this motivation was not correctly channeled, I could end up damaging my chances for success at an early age. Realizing this, I've succeeded so far in pushing my desire for the opposite sex into business. This quote from movie *Scarface* really helped:

"In this country, you gotta make the money first. Then when you get the money, you get the power. Then when you get the power, then you get the woman."
- Al Pacino, in Scareface

Having this quote in front of me has helped me put all of the desire I have for sex and love into business. Think of all of the time, effort, and money some people put into attracting the opposite sex. Imagine if that desire went into planning how to be successful in real estate! This time last year I was trying to meet the person with the hottest girls around; now I am looking for the guy who has access to the most investment opportunities. The same amount of effort but double the benefits. Look inside yourself and figure out what really motivates you, than apply that toward real estate. With that slight shift in motivation, it will be easy to have self-control.

The Value of Real Estate Courses
February 1, 2005

When you're first starting out, you have to review as many real estate courses as you can. It's beneficial to take a course; however, they are expensive, so find someone with a course and borrow it. I have gotten courses from my mentor and swapped courses with people I've met at the REIA meeting. I have personally studied more than $100,000 worth of educational material and attended several three-day classes. These courses go into more detail than anyone ever could in a book.

A course will usually include 6 to 12 CDs, some DVDs, forms, programs, and access to speak with a real estate guru for a certain amount of time. If you do not have the funds, do what you can to save/borrow the money. Trust me; you will pay for your education one way or another. It feels a lot better to pay for education than lose money on an investment.

> "An investment in knowledge always pays
> the best interest."
> –Ben Franklin

Most people who put as much emphasis as I am doing on buying a course are actually trying to sell you one. Please take this as an unbiased opinion because I do not have a course to sell you. I have personally learned a great deal from the courses I have reviewed. If your mentor is providing all of your knowledge, he or she may purposely leave out certain important pieces of information to make sure you keep on working for him or her; the course won't do that. Education is everything in real estate. In this field you will never stop learning.

Looking back: As I mentioned earlier, I attended a three-day training seminar on investing in real estate. It was not until four years after originally writing this section that I remembered the other students' reactions. The other students attending the seminar were all at least 15 years my senior, with an average age of about 45. I remember people coming over to me, praising me for being at the seminar, telling me how rich I was going to be and how they wished they had known this information when they were my age. Everyone was so sure I was going to attain all of my goals, and that encouragement empowered me. It motivated me and gave me the confidence I needed to keep pushing. Go to a training seminar; the inspiration it will give you will be worth every dollar.

Homework: Find two or three day investment training. Also, find someone who will let you borrow a real estate course on just about any topic. Not a book, a full course with many training manuals, audio, forms, etc. Course/ training suggestions: Subject to investing, short sales, private money, wholesaling, or lease options. Eventually, you will need to become an expert on each of these topics.

Chapter 7—Building Momentum

"The big shots are only the little shots that kept shooting."— Christopher Morley, *Business Inspiration Quotes*

Building a Team Starts With Building a Dream
February 15, 2005

Once you are able to speak intelligently about investing in real estate, you will be able to build the dream in other people. If you do not honestly have the dream of rising to royalty through real estate, it will be next to impossible to build it in someone else. Building this dream in other people is very important. If someone has a burning inner desire to change their life with real estate and believes you will play a key role in their success, you will be able to make thousands of dollars through their efforts. This type of relationship is great because you can point them in a direction that provides a mutually beneficial relationship. By channeling my desire my mentor has built so much wealth for himself, it's truly remarkable.

You need to speak to everyone you know about real estate. Always let them see how excited you are and share with them successes of yourself or others. When you build the dream in others, they are more likely to help you with your rise to royalty. Just like how I appeared out of nowhere and made my mentor John hundreds of thousands of dollars in only six months. If you're actively chasing leads every day, the people you will work with will fall out of the sky, do whatever you need, and make you a lot of money, as long as you can build and reinforce the opportunity they have working with you.

When I first started working with John, I didn't receive one dollar from him for five months. If John hadn't constantly reinforced the dream, I would have never been able to stay on track. Now that I have been through approximately 14 real estate investments with John and have been doing this full-time for six months, people are starting to come to me, asking if they can work with me. I have a lot of people in their twenties, just out of college, wanting to help me. I have also had people in their forties ask if they can work with me. At first this feels weird. But I will work with anyone who wants to get paid commission; I have nothing to lose.

Being Young and Investing in Real Estate
February 16, 2005

"Options—the ability to choose—is real power."—Tim Ferriss, *The 4-Hour Work Week*

It is great being young in the real estate game because of the amazing number of options you have. Since it often takes time to establish yourself in this business, one of the best things about being young is you generally don't have the stress of having to make money to support a family yet. (It took more than 18 months for real estate investing to put money in my pocket.) Other benefits of being young include people constantly praising you for what you are doing, which adds to your confidence. More successful investors are willing to mentor you and/or give you advice because they don't see you as a threat; you're just a kid. You can play dumb to draw information out of anyone. One of the benefits I have enjoyed is that everyone remembers me: "Yeah, the young kid; I know him."

If you are young and ambitious, people will remember you. If you're a young and ambitious woman, I believe even more people will remember you. The best thing about getting into real estate investing young is that you can retire young. I'm sure you remember the example I used earlier in the book about your super power: compounded interest. It is such an important lesson; let's take a look at that quote again:

"Compounded interest is the most powerful force in the universe."—Albert Einstein

If you buy a $100,000 dollar home today for $70,000, rent the home out for 10 years—in my market—history proves 10 years of appreciation will more than double your money. You should easily be able to sell that same house for at least $200,000. Wouldn't it be nice to start off at age 20, and buy one house every two years? At 30, you're selling one house every two years, making $100,000 plus—even if you never get off your couch. By the time you're 40, you have over a million dollars.

I hope everyone who picked up this book was doing so to become a millionaire, because there is your plan. Get excited; you can do it. This plan is simple and proven, and I guarantee you, if you put this book down today and come back to it in 10 years, you will wish you had bought real estate.

Chapter 8—Starts and Stalls
on the Road to Royalty

"'The more money you have, the more problems you have' is not just a quote by rapper Biggie Smalls."

Once You Realize You Have Money
April 27, 2005

I have finally come to the exciting realization that I have money. For so long I saved every dollar. Before I had money, the only problem I had was how to get money. Now that I have it, though, the issues get more complicated. Once you start showing income, you have to deal with the one partner you will be learning how to deal with for the rest of your life: Uncle Sam. This is the family member you can't shake.

Taxes become an issue when you have money, and the main thing you have to consider is how much income you want to show. Show a lot of income and pay a lot of taxes; don't show enough income, and it will be hard to qualify for loans. You must have a plan for how to spend the money you make efficiently. Get an accountant and pay the $75 to $150 a month to have a bookkeeper. My accountant constantly reminds me of where I stand and what I need to do and makes sure if the IRS ever audits my business I have top-notch records. Due to the many ways you can use real estate to offset earnings, real estate investors are among one of the top individuals to be audited.

Using Religion
July 10, 2005

I cannot help but notice the business people who use religion in their marketing. In real estate, you have to build rapport with your clients. I have watched many business people use religion to gain trust from people. It seems only natural to use this approach if religion is a huge part of your life. I have seen investors get phone calls solely because they used the term "God bless" in their marketing. If you can find a way to instantly gain people's trust and you feel comfortable, go with it. Church can be a great place to start your network.

Once You Realize You Don't Have Money!
July 25, 2005

The good news is, I just purchased a primary residence worth $254,000 for $138,000! The bad news is, it cost me everything I had and then some. Just last month I had closed on several investments that instantly made me money, and I had other homes in the pipeline. This month my quick money is coming a little slower. What really got me was a deal that seemed as good as done, was far from it. This deal was going to make me some great quick money—and it fell through. I had a nice chunk of money in savings, but I had to buy this home ASAP. My credit score is looking bad because of all the recent transactions. To get this deal, I promised the seller a closing in 30 days and put *time is of the essence* on the contract. I just can't get around this home costing me a ton of money to close.

In retrospect, I should have taken it easy on impulse buys and vacations. I also spent thousands on my business and advertising. This is the first time I've ever had real money. I'm a single, 22-year-old guy and have thousands of dollars coming to me every week, and I felt like I deserved some things for all my hard work.The house I just purchased took all of my money to close. I now have a grand total of $38 in the bank. This is not a good feeling when you have a $1,200 credit card bill, $5,000 in repairs, and $2,000 in other monthly bills due in the next two weeks.

Promise me this: When you find yourself making money in real estate within the first year and you quit your day job, keep some good reserves in the bank. Real estate can pull just as much money out of your pocket as it can put in, and it always seems to come in waves.

If I don't qualify for an equity line of credit, I will be in a huge financial mess.

Learning From My Mistakes
August 1, 2005

My lack of experience, plus the fact that I was only listening to what I wanted to hear, caused me to overlook some key issues. I did not plan correctly and have been denied by everyone for my equity line. Because it was so difficult to qualify for my loan to purchase the house, my credit was checked so many times, it has hit an all-time low of a 630. No one could get me refinanced. They all want to see six months' seasoning on my loan. *Shit.* Excuse my language; however, I need to pool together $5,000 just to pay my bills. To put it plain and simple, I am in financial trouble. I can only hope all my tenants pay on time, and I'll be able to close on some decent deals ASAP. I heard that when a man's is broke, his true character will always show. This is my opportunity to prove to myself I can cope with stress.

Just to give you an idea of how broke I am: It's August in North Carolina and I'm driving around with my AC off to save gas, my new girlfriend is feeding me, and I owe my parents $1,600. If I can make it through all of this, I will have more than $100,000 in my bank account. Right now I'm looking for roommates, hoping to collect first month's rent and deposit.

"If cash is king, then credit is queen, and we all know the queen can have a huge influence on what the king can achieve."

Take care of your credit today! Although there are ways around bad credit, it will be like oiling the joints of your business if you improve your credit score. If you don't know what your credit score is, or if you know you have bad credit, start to work on raising your score today.

Another lesson I learned from this: Only take advice from someone who has been in the business for a long time. My mortgage broker assured me he would be able to get me refinanced ASAP. That loan was my financial life jacket; right now I'm treading water in the financial ocean. I'm balance-transferring my credit card bills and eating ramen noodles.

Looking back: *Because of my financial difficulties during this time in my life, I was forced to review my actions. Learn from my mistakes. Do not get cocky when you get your first few hits. Also, educate yourself on what affects a credit score.*

I may have jumped the gun on hiring an accountant however, it is very important to keep extremely accurate records of your business transactions, and I was pretty clueless when it came to accounting at the time.

Research: *Understand the amazing tax benefits of being an investor. A good place to start is reviewing the book: "Loopholes of the rich" By Diane Kennedy*

Chapter 9—The 180 Look Back

This is my personal favorite quote.

"Divine power, I ask not for more riches but more wisdom to make use of the riches you gave me at birth consisting of the power to control and direct my mind to whatever ends I desire."—Napoleon Hill

Family and Friends
August 15, 2005

Family and friends are priceless. If you haven't already learned this valuable lesson, investing in real estate young could help you realize how much you should appreciate those relationships. My rise to royalty would be much more painful if it weren't for my family and friends. Right here I want to sincerely thank the people who have been there for me when I had nothing to offer but my gratitude. My dad and I have been fixing up my new house together every weekend. My mom has been helping as much as she can. My uncles have spent some time helping me, and my girlfriend has put up with me being totally broke.

Credit
September 28, 2005

The more you dive into real estate, the more the issue of credit will come up. To put things in perspective for you: Trying to be a real estate investor with bad credit is like being a boxer with a sprained wrist. But if you do not have good credit it's nothing to be ashamed of (only 2 percent of Americans have a credit score of 750 or better), and it should never stop you from diving into real estate. You can always use someone else's credit.

If you apply for a loan on a $100,000 home and receive an interest rate 1 percent lower because of good credit, you will save approximately $30,000 over the course of a 30-year loan! Your credit should be something you take very seriously and constantly monitor and improve.

Dealing With Young Professionals
October 11, 2005

I feel like a hypocrite writing this section; however, this is a lesson you need to learn from someone else's mistake. Don't deal with professionals who have been in the business for fewer than five years. I'm talking about mortgage brokers, accountants, appraisers, attorneys, laborers, and anyone else. I wish someone had told me this couple of years ago; I would have avoided taking bad advice from many different young professionals.

It is only natural for you to make young friends who are mortgage brokers and real estate agents, but don't give them your business. Refer them as much business as possible; let them learn on someone else's portfolio. The young professionals will obviously seem the most outgoing and give you all the "Yeah, I can do that; no problem" answers, but nothing will ever get the job done like experience. What I've learned is that people who are extremely hungry for commission will drag you along as long as possible. You need people who can give you the most valuable advice: hindsight. We have all heard the expression "Time is money." Let's put things in a different light: "Your time is your money." I will no longer give my business to anyone who has not been in his or her field for less than five years.

Reputations
February 15, 2006

A reputation is like a castle of cards: difficult and time-consuming to build, and one wrong move and it's all gone.

In the real estate world, reputation is a very important tool. If you upset the wrong person, your 10-story card castle can be leveled. I am learning this from a safe distance. There have been certain situations where individuals I have given my business to have looked me in the eyes and lied directly to my face. I am going to be in the real estate world for a very long time, so one of these individuals just lost tens of thousands of dollars of repeat business and a lifetime of referrals. Actually, the same day this individual lied to me I had more than six people stop working with him, and two of those individuals were millionaires.

If you tell someone you are going to do something, you must follow through—even if you're going to make a little less money today. It will be worth it in the long run.

"To speak the truth in every instance; give nobody expectations that are not likely to be answered, but aim at sincerity in every word and action." — Ben Franklin

Something That Can Be a Lot of Fun!
April 10, 2006

Because the most important part of any real estate deal is the financing, you must focus on building relationships with wealthy people who will want to work with you as private investors. This is one of the most important steps in your young real estate career, and it was my New Year's resolution for this year. You can never know too many millionaires. I believe at least 50 percent of your time should be dedicated to finding the people with the money.

Once you have access to millions of other people's money, you will feel like you've gained a special power. You now have the power of money. I am 23 years old and I have access to $10,000,000.

I want you to do something for me right now. Put the book down, take a deep breath, close your eyes, and very slowly, say "ten million dollars." How did that feel? It's very hard for most people to say "ten million dollars" without a smile on their face.

Being 23 years old with access to that type of money is an accomplishment in itself. I can access those funds in 48 hours. The main restriction is I can only use that money to put a 60 percent first mortgage on a property. Meaning if a property is worth 100,000, I can only borrow 60,000 to purchase the property.

For me, getting access to these funds has been fun. While everyone else my age was getting told what to do by their boss, I was hanging out on a yacht on a Tuesday afternoon—drinking a Crown and Coke, talking business. If you are young and a wealthy individual says; "This kid reminds me of myself," you know you're "in."

Everyone and their mom would like to invest in undervalued real estate, but most people do not have the time. After you've invested your time and your smarts in setting up a good marketing campaign, this business is only as time-consuming as you want it to be. I can't tell you how to find the people with money in your town; however, usually all you have to do is ask. Some of the terminology we are about to cover might be over your head. I am purposely not going into detail here because I could write an entire book just on this one technique; however, this will give you the direction you need to start asking the questions that will find you a ton of wealthy individuals who enjoy passively investing in real estate.

Search for self-directed IRAs that are the grantee on a deed of trust created within the last 24 months. The beneficiary named in these docs will be your private lender. You will find an address; do a reverse address search to find telephone info and once you have a deal give the person a call. Prior to contacting a potential private lender, you need to make sure you have all of your ducks in a row—appraisal, inspection, and a good exit strategy.

If someone has money sitting around and they believe you can find them real estate investments at 60 percent of the value, there is no reason for them not to say. "Okay, kid; bring me a deal." If you are associated with enough successful people, success will rub off on you. Networking with millionaires will help you in many different ways. You will understand that most of these millionaires are nothing special. They may offer you opportunities you never dreamed of. Make someone a quick $30,000 and they'll not only love you, they'll brag about you.

My favorite feeling is when I sit down with a millionaire, look him in the eyes, and I fully believe—and know—that I will be more successful than he is by the time I'm his age. This is how I level the playing field in my mind, and that's all that matters.

Never Stop Learning
April 20, 2006

We are all aware of the saying "knowledge is power." You made a decision when you opened this book to gain what power you could from the lessons herein. Never stop acquiring power. You can never know everything about real estate; however, your goal should be to try. A book will explain what you will be up against and give you motivation. Keep in mind, though, that all a book can really do is get you excited and point you in the right direction. Never stop learning; you can always improve on what you're doing. Set aside time for research. Just as real estate agents routinely have to take a certain number of continuing education courses as a requirement for keeping their real estate license, you need to do the same. There are hundreds of courses available. I strongly recommend reviewing a few full real estate courses.

I am simply opening your eyes to how big your rise to royalty could be. If you are like me, you were looking for real estate investing books because you wanted to learn how to make an extra $40,000. I'm telling you that once you apply this knowledge, the world will open more doors for you than you ever thought existed. You will have so much opportunity, you will be able to pick and choose how you want to make money.

Fire!
May 22, 2006

This morning I received a phone call. My rental house caught on fire! The tenants left the stove on, and now I have to deal with the rebuilding of a kitchen. Thank God for homeowners insurance! The only real problem here is that my renters do not have renters' insurance, meaning I have to sue the renter to get the money out of him. If he had rental insurance, I could get the money for repairs from his insurance company

May 23, 2006

Since my renters did not have renters insurance, my insurance company will be suing them for the thousands of dollars in damages. There is $18,000 worth of damages. That $18,000 is what it would cost if I had the top contractors come in and fix everything. I don't want my tenants to have to pay $18,000 for something that can be fixed for less, so I told the insurance company I would accept $10,000 if they do not file a claim against my tenant. The insurance company happily agreed. I am paying for materials, and in this case, fortunately, the homeowner is very handy, so I am having him do all the work.

What seemed like a bad situation will give me a new kitchen and raise the value of my home. I love real estate.

I Am the Mentor
May 25, 2006

It has been about 20 months since I took on my mentor. The apprentice is now a mentor to others. This will happen to you as well. Reading the earlier sections in this book, I see that the day I took on a mentor, I somehow already knew that I myself would become a mentor in the near future. One day I would be viewed as an expert in my field, and people would come to me for my knowledge. I know how to make money in real estate, and that's what people want to learn. That's why you are reading this book. But I still don't feel like an expert because the more you learn, the more you realize you don't know. To me, real estate investing is an endless journey of education and skill-sharpening.

Looking back: *This section is significant because it was a time of action. I was taking calculated risks, building my reputation, finding money, dealing with fire. People were intrigued by my passion and energy. This lead to invitations to speak at local events. Now I speak on national stages and invest all around the United States. I can trace the seed of my success back to the first time I attended my local real estate investment association.*

One of the most important actions I ever took was dedicating a large amount of my energy to finding and networking with wealthy individuals.

Homework: *Visit ConnectedInvestors.com and sign up with promo code –Ross. Once you are in, the system will tell you what to do.*

Chapter 11—Taking Off the Training Wheels

"The young do not know enough to be prudent, and therefore, they attempt the impossible—and achieve it, generation after generation."—Pearl S. Buck

April 20, 2007

"Becoming a millionaire is like trying to lift a million pounds. It's only possible with proper leverage."

Once you have worked with a mentor for a while, you will start to gain the most valuable aspect of a real estate investing career: experience. I have seen how hundreds of real estate transactions played out, from "We just made $500,000" to "We just lost $50,000." I have advised you to work with a mentor and help him or her find profitable investments. If you do this, you will eventually have a system in place to find good investments. Watching these deals go from leads to profits using other people's money (OPM), you will gain experience. When speaking with other investors, you will be able to hold a good conversation, speak intelligently about past investments, and compare notes.

Now that you have experience and a good source of leads coming in, it is time to learn how to "cherry pick." If you get a phone call about someone wanting to sell a home, instead of simply passing it to your mentor as you've done in the past, analyze the deal for yourself. If it looks good, do it yourself. If something about the deal is not working for you, pass it on to other investors and watch how it goes from the sideline. Cherry picking will allow you to always take a step in the right direction.

Throughout history, a business that sustains success has used the *crawl, walk, run* strategy. However, in real estate after *run* comes *ride!*

Crawl: Find a mentor. Learn everything you can from him or her, and build experience and a team. Learn how and why your mentor is successful, and then improve on what he or she does.

Walk: Cherry pick. Do a couple of deals yourself. At this point you are still working with your investors; you should have about five investors you work with by now.

Run: Once a couple of your cherry picked deals close and you deposit $50,000 in the bank, you will not need to work with other investors. However, if you're smart, you will still have good relationships. Now, instead of being a bird dog, you and your investors will have LLCs set up and you will partner on deals.

Ride: The ride part of real estate is why I got involved. Once your real estate is set up properly (and you will learn what *properly* means to you throughout the process), your real estate will take care of you in so many ways.

So get excited, you have a lot of fun ahead. Make things happen, and you can live and invest with no worries. Every morning when I wake up, my primary goal is to learn about money and how to properly invest. When I invest, my funds are always secured by a lot of equity and has a 20 percent+ ROI, worst-case scenario. No matter what the stock market does, my money is safe. For me to lose money, housing would have to drop 50 percent overnight. And if that happens, I will probably have more important things to worry about, like a depression across the country.

(A quick look back: Once the US housing bubble popped, some areas saw 70% decreases in property values. Luckily, my area was not hit that hard)

Everyone has seen the infomercials on how to make millions in real estate. Their processes may or may not be correct, but the concept is right in line with: "You don't build your real estate portfolio to rest on; you use your heightened elevation, locate opportunities and jump to the next level of wealth."

Misunderstanding an Important Feeling
April 16, 2007

If you ever feel like you need to "save money," I hope you spend some time analyzing your motivation. What problem will saving money solve? How much do you hope to save? What are you going to "give up" to achieve this goal of saving money? Giving up something always seems to be the solution. The real solution is that you need to give up saving.

Today, if you are saving money in an account that does not give you at least 6 percent interest, you're losing money every day. Match that fact up with your motivation and what you hope to solve by saving money. You will easily realize you're moving in the wrong direction.

If you are actually able to save money, there is hope. You are doing better than 95 percent of Americans. The last statistic that I read on the national saving average was that "the average American spends 1.11 dollars to every dollar earned." Don't get excited because you're in the top 5 percent. You do not want to compare yourself to the masses of America when it comes to money management; it's not a fair comparison. Unless I'm missing something huge, the American government cannot even manage its money. Why do you think your dollar is falling so fast?

Using America from any angle of comparison would be like being in a school for the mentally incapable and bragging because you're one of the best students. Comparing yourself to the national average is like being pleased with making a passing grade in a school with teachers who couldn't even pass the tests they are giving. You need only compare yourself with the rich. That feeling of needing to save money is tricking your mind.

"The frustration of not knowing how to advantageously invest often comes disguised in the feeling of needing to save money."

Quick Flips Suck

The first question I ask someone wanting to work with me is, "What are you looking for in a real estate investment?" and the answer I get every time is: "I want to flip homes." It's okay to think that way. Most real estate books are marketed toward making millions by quickly buying and selling real estate. What I am going to introduce to you here is a new reality, in which the first step to becoming rich is changing your perception. So we're going to pause, take a deep breath, and stand back so we can get a look at the bigger picture. Once you've read this section, you will hate selling any home you own.

You want to quick-flip homes, then what? Think about that for at least a couple of seconds. Then...what...? After you make your millions in real estate by "flipping homes," what are you going to do? Your taxes will be 33 percent of your income, you will lose most of your tax write-offs, and most importantly—you will *lose* the power owning real estate provides.

Consider this scenario: I leverage myself so well that one day, I own all the real estate in the country. I own every parcel of land from New York to California. Who has more leverage——me or the guy with a billion dollars *cash?* Weapons aside, who has more power—me or the government? No one can stop me from raising rents, and if it weren't for the law of eminent domain, I would have complete control. In many countries, foreigners—and sometimes even locals—can never own the land; they are only allowed to lease it. Many smaller countries realized long ago that if citizens of a wealthy country buy a large part of their land, those landowners will have too much power. *Real estate is power.*

Most quick-turn real estate investors don't understand that real estate is more than money, it is leverage. Real estate is one of the very few tools available that can enable you to achieve magic: Spend some time learning and find a really great deal, use no money, and become a millionaire.

Let's look at my second home:

I bought the home for $138,000 with no money down. Within 30 days I had the rooms in the house rented, so the home was not costing me one dollar. Six months later, appraised value was $254,000 and I still had no money in the deal. I pulled out over $25,000 cash and set up an $85,000 equity line.

Fast forward to the present: I have leveraged just that one equity line into many other homes. I have equity lines on the other homes to buy other homes. Are you starting to see the power in the buy and hold? Theoretically, I will become a multimillionaire simply by correctly leveraging one real estate deal in which I have no money. So many people want to get into real estate to make quick money. Holding real estate is power. This book is subtitled *Rise to Royalty.* Other than money, what comes with royalty? Power.

Guess where I got the money to publish and market this book?

> **Looking back:** *So many people worry about saving money for retirement. Once you have a nice portfolio built you will no longer have to "save money." Instead, you will have to manage your portfolio of properties you are holding. There is nothing wrong with selling homes; however, that is not the definition of being wealthy. Some homes you will buy to resell; some homes you will buy to hold. Once you start to feel the crawl-walk-run-ride, the momentum will take over and you will know you will be able to take care of yourself and your family forever.*

Chapter 12—Should I Get a Real Estate License?

"If you want to show kitchens get your license; if you want to make money learn how to invest in real estate."—John Long

To Be a Realtor or Not to Be; That Is the Question
May 19, 2007

If you are getting into real estate, deciding whether or not to be a Realtor may become a question. What is the answer? As you may or may not recall, this is the very first question I asked my mentor, so let's take a step into memory lane and go back to August 17, 2004, when I wrote the following:

I just had to ask a pro his opinion about the necessity of having a real estate license.

I interrupted John's conversation and asked "Just starting out, should I get my real estate license so I can become familiar with buying and selling houses?"

After the laughter faded from the group of older investors standing in a circle, John answered: "Do you want to show kitchens or make money?"

Obviously, I replied, "I want to make money."

He told me to buy options on houses and wholesale them to people at the REIA meeting.

It is 100 percent true that you do not need a Realtor license to rise to royalty, and not having your license will keep your mind in the right direction. Having a license may make it easier for you to take your eye off the original goal of rising to royalty through real estate investing. Having a license puts you under the microscope on every transaction you make, and signs you up to vexatious laws and processes you *must* follow that will limit your flexibility.

In retrospect, looking back over the last couple of years, I realize that if I'd had a license, I could have made some nice commission checks. It would have been one more stream of income when times were slow. Every book I have ever read that gets into this topic states a different opinion, and they never give you the answer. Well, I have the exact answer you need. Let's go over some of the benefits of a license, and then review some of the situations I have been in but found myself unable to maximize my profit because I didn't have a license:

1. Save money on taxes. If you list a home and sell it, you can charge yourself a commission of up to 10 percent. Profit on the sale of a property is taxed up to 33 percent. Income earned off a commission is ordinary income and the taxes are less than half. This is an easy, clean way to save money on capital gains tax.

2. Access to the MLS. To put it bluntly, you need access to the MLS. It's getting harder and harder every year to get access without a license. Six months ago, all I needed was an access code to pull values on a home. Now Realtors get key chains that have a digital code. This digital code changes every two minutes, and it has made it a pain in the ass to get in the MLS site, which is something I need every day. In the near future, they will probably have finger or eye scans.

3. The legal right to charge commissions to sell other people's properties. On more than one occasion I have found myself in the middle of a multimillion dollar deal. It is hard to tie up and flip a property of that size without a substantial, nonrefundable down payment. If you are going to try to pass a very large deal to another investor and you do not have an equitable interest in the property, the only thing you can try to do is put a consulting agreement together. Again, a big pain, besides which any consulting agreement you put together is nowhere near as enforceable as a Realtor contract. If you're in front of a judge and you've got a Realtor contract, you win; if you've only got a consulting agreement, you *might* win.

Sometimes you will refer *big* business to a Realtor, and without a license it is very difficult to get a kickback. The main reason for this is because it's illegal and the Realtor can lose his or her license. Don't get me wrong; most Realtors will discreetly give cash kickbacks, but they are nowhere near the monetary size a commission split would be.

These are the only reasons I have ever contemplated having a license. So what is the answer for people like us, who want it all? This solution may not be a "today" answer for everyone, but it is the only answer that gets you the best of both worlds: Have your significant other get their license. Now you can play whatever role you want. If you need the Realtor commission, put the whole deal together and have your significant other step in once it's done. He or she will be very happy to earn all this extra money. Now you just have to convince him or her to take the classes and the test.

Looking back: *To get a license or not get a license? Although the answer I outline is a great solution, there is no correct answer to this question. One thing I can answer for sure is, if you have your business properly set up you will not want to bother with all of the red tape a license brings with it. It all has to do with your mind frame. Do you want to be an investor or a real estate agent? At first it does not seem like there are big differences, however the life styles of each professional will be completely unique. Although I have passed the class, to this day I still have never activated a real estate license.*

Chapter 13—Keep Your Eyes Open

"Sometimes we're on a collision course, and we just don't know it."—
Brad Pitt, from *The Curious Case of Benjamin Button*

If It Walks Like a Duck and Sounds Like a Duck, It's a Duck
May 19, 2007

I'm sure you have heard the title of this section before. However, when I was in a situation where this quote could have saved me a lot of time and money, for some reason I decided to ignore the little voice in the back of my head repeating that bit of wisdom more than a few times.

I have been encouraging you to work with a mentor and split the profit once a property sells. This is great if the investor pays. In the actual situation I'm talking about, I was working with an investor who told me, "I don't work with people who need contracts. I don't work with people who don't trust me, and I don't trust people if they insist on a contract." Well, that's the walk-and-talk part. When push came to shove, he paid me one-fifth of what we had agreed on. This put me in a bind because I had promised another partner a certain dollar amount in this transaction.

Just because my investor did not honor his word did not mean I was going to back out of my commitment. I paid him every dollar I had promised. The deal cost me $500. But it is so important to keep people bringing you properties, don't bite (or be cheap to) the hand that feeds you. The lesson is, of course, that you must always get an agreement in writing up front. This agreement must include what you are going to do and what they are going to do.

Take It to the Next Level
July 7, 2007

The previous entry in this book is what gave me the little extra push to take it to the next level. I had made my mentor a millionaire many times over and had made another gentleman about $150,000 in two months. I then had to take a step back and figure out what was holding me back. It was, very simply, fear—the fear of loss. Fear of loss accounts for 70 percent of your motivation, whereas the drive to gain only accounts for 30 percent. So let's turn this around and put the fear in our favor.

What if my life changes and I never have another opportunity to buy and sell real estate? I will have to become a slave—I mean, get a "real job." That is truly my worst fear, to have to work nine to five for someone else. I don't care if my job is to rub lotion on swimsuit models; in my mind having a traditional boss means giving up a part of your freedom. There is a little switch inside us all that will give us the confidence to move toward what we want. For me, that switch was having my partners screw me out of well over $50,000. I was only mad at myself for not properly capitalizing on the opportunities that had crossed my path.

It has been a few years since then; I have seen it done, understand what the bottom line will be, and what it will take to get there. I have the relationships built, the confidence, and the available funds; it's time to rise to royalty.

What is the best way to buy real estate now that you are using your own money? I have now been a part of hundreds of transactions, so let's reflect on what works and why. First off, we have to figure out what we want at this stage of the game. Let's start with a best-case scenario: We want low risk and high reward, we want to have cash flow every month and if we need to raise funds, it is nice to have the opportunity to sell. We also want the ability to borrow against the properties we take control of in order to leverage the equity into other investments. Most importantly, we want full control, don't want the properties to show on our credit, and don't want to use much cash. Also, it would be nice if we did not have to do a lot of repairs to the properties. Is this possible? We will find out in the next few pages.

If you knew for a fact you could not fail, wouldn't you pull together every dollar you could to invest? If I knew I could not fail I would take out equity lines; borrow money from credit cards, family, and friends; and pull all my cash together and invest. You can't lose, so you might as well go all in. The investment I am about to introduce is so good right now that the government is trying to make it illegal.

If you have available funds, whether it's cash, equity, or money you can borrow from anyone, you need to put it to work. Having money not working would be like having a healthy 25-year-old sleeping on his parents' couch every day. You would probably give him a look of disgust and ask, "Why you don't do something with your life?" When I see money just sitting there, I look at it the same way. It makes me sick to see $20,000 just sitting there watching reruns of *Seinfeld* and taking up space. Plus it's bad for the economy to hold all your money.

Once you have at least $10,000 available to invest, you need to get your money working for you because the type of investment I am about to introduce to you to is almost like predicting the future.

Here are the basic details of an investment I am closing on this week:

I am taking $4,874 and cash flowing $150 a month. That is over a 30 percent ROI. If a month goes by and I do not receive my 30 percent, I have the opportunity to make $70,000. Let's go back over what we want in an investment and see if the investment strategy I am using checks out:

1.   Low risk, check

2.   High reward, check

3.   Cash flow every month, check

4.   The opportunity for a flip, check

5.   Borrow against it, check

6.   Not on my credit, check

7.   Full control, check

8.   Not much cash up front, check

9.   Repairs, on this house just paint and carpet, check

After doing one of these transactions from start to finish you will
need a cold glass of water, it's that good.   I included a picture of my friend Grey cashing a $34,000.00 check he earned using this technique.   Grey lives on the beach, surfs about every day, travels, and always has a smile on his face. He flips a few deals like this each year allowing him to enjoy life without a traditional J.O.B.

Sounds like we found ourselves an investment strategy, the *subject to*. I am not even going to give you the definition of a *subject to*. I want you to be motivated to buy a course on this topic. No matter how long you have been investing, you need to fully understand how to use the subject to if you want to quickly rise to royalty. I use the *subject to* as my buy and hold strategy. Every time I structure a *subject to* I make sure I am going to see at least 30 percent return on investment in the first year. You can easily do the same.

The main reason I recommend understanding the ins and outs of *subject to* investing is because it provides an amazing amount of leverage and in most cases you do not have to get a loan in your name. Why buy the cow when you can get the milk for free.

Currently, the government is trying to make *subject to* investing illegal—that's how good it is. If *subject to* investing is still legal by the time this book is published, I recommend purchasing (or borrowing) a *subject to* course. You can't afford to be cheap right now; it does not take money to make money, it takes applied specialized knowledge and persistence. You might say, "But I need money to buy the course to learn the specialized knowledge." Not if you're persistent. If you let that stop you, then I'm going to save you a lot of headache and tell you right now, you don't have what it takes, and I strongly recommend not getting into real estate investing.

If You Think It Can't Happen, Think Again

In real estate investing, there is a lot of money to be made—obviously. Hundreds, thousands, millions, billions can all be made through investing in real estate. Once you learn how to turn $5,000 into $10,000, it is only a matter of time mixed with determination before you are presented with the opportunity to turn $500,000 into $1,000,000, and so on. The point I am trying to make is that it is easy to get greedy in real estate. Greed or being desperate can easily take over a person's logical decision-making process, causing an investor to cross the line of legality to grab profits. I have seen it occur many times. I have been in direct contact with people who have crossed the line so far that some sort of death seemed to overcome them. Personal friends of mine have had their lives threatened. I have bought houses from people who forged and recorded deeds. Associates of mine have let the greed take over their decision-making process and had literally stolen people's homes. This has all happened in the last three years. Although I only dedicated about half a page to the topic of reputations, an entire book could be written on the importance of maintaining a good reputation.

Mr. Alvin (Name changed to protect the privacy of his family)

My deepest condolences go out to the great family this individual left behind.

When I first started working in real estate, I started searching for all the financial advisors in my town that would take the time to sit down with an individual who was young, motivated, and broke. One professional I spoke with was David Alvin. David had a radio show on investing and seemed to be a good guy. We had a long "What would you do if you were me?" conversation. Ultimately, he tried to coerce me out of $4,000 to set up a Roth IRA and a corporation. The IRA was good advice, but I was able to set one up myself for next to nothing. He did own a large amount of real estate and had the resources in place to pull together large amount of funds for real estate investment opportunities. I was not happy with him;

however, I wanted to maintain good standing with David in case I needed to leverage his resources.

David had everything you need to be credible. He had been in the service, married for many years, and had a family. Also, being the host of a respected radio show for years gave David all the credibility a crook needs. One particular deal of David's involved a huge "Investors Offering" he was advertising for a $50,000,000 project he was putting together. He had done a very efficient job of pulling in the money he needed from big and small investors to get it off the ground.

I knew he was putting this project together and was getting close to breaking ground. He had most of the necessary approvals from the city in place, as well as the money needed for the initial push of the project. Once this project was completed, David would be a very, very rich man. One of the lessons I live by is that every multimillionaire you associate yourself with improves your chance of success. Two years after our initial meeting, I set up an appointment with David. We spoke for a couple of hours, and things went well. By the end of the conversation he was trying to set his daughter and me up on a date. She was an attractive, wealthy massage therapist. I digress on this only to point out that I was—and still am—in a committed relationship. We decided that instead of dating his daughter, I would help him raise money for his project.

Within 45 days I had raised over $90,000 for his project. These investors were not extremely wealthy individuals; they were families in their mid-forties who were planning on retiring in one of the condos to be built. I almost invested in the project myself, but since I had so many other investments at the time, I decided just to watch the project take shape.

Judging by the title of this section, you can tell there is a twist. This is not a happy-ending story. Approximately five months ago, David was arrested for tax evasion. This caused a widespread panic among the investors in his project; however, he was able to calm most of them down. What could the investors do? They had no control over this real estate investment. They had to hope things would turn out in their favor. Three months ago, a very savvy and successful local lawyer who wanted to bury David organized a class action suit. David did not keep his word on any of the contracts with his investors in the project, many of whom were now being questioned by the FBI. The biggest question as the project began to slowly crumble was: Where's the money?

David was facing a very long prison sentence. I had seen some investor information on the project. There were many people who had invested over $1,000,000. There is a good chance he stole from the wrong person. Shortly after this issue surfaced, David was flying his plane and a mechanical failure caused the plane to crash. David perished.

Was it karma, murder, or suicide? Whatever was the cause of David's death, there is a lesson to be learned other than the one karma provided. Real estate investing can be risky; however, one of the main benefits of investing in real estate is that you have control over your investment. Be careful in situations where you have no control. If you want a hands-off type real estate investment, good luck—and get a lawyer's opinion of the paperwork. If you have a gut feeling something is not right, put your money elsewhere.

Live to Fight Another Day

Moving into the land side of real estate, I associated myself with a gentleman named Dave, a successful investor in his early thirties. He specialized in very large land acquisitions. My friend would often locate patently profitable properties through the Internet, GIS, or word of mouth. Before negotiating with the owners, he would often walk the property just to get an idea of what he might be able to do with the land.

In early 2003, there was a large area of land about to rise substantially in value. This land was considered a hot commodity by everyone who had an inside track. One day, as Dave was walking through the woods, he just happened to run into another group of land acquisitionists. In this area they were know as the Mafia. They had purchased a very large amount of land in the area in the late 1900s, and as you know, whoever owns the land makes the rules.

My friend Dave tried to pretend he was a hunter looking for a spot to build a tree stand, but the group of guys knew better. They made it very clear to Dave that if he or anyone he knew tried to purchase the land he was walking, he would not be able to walk for a long time. After some juvenile shoving and intimidation, they let Dave go on his way. Realizing he would be better off to live to fight another day, Dave never put in an offer on the land. A short time after this run-in, the aforementioned group of "acquisitionists" purchased the land, and surprisingly, no other offers were made.

Incidentally, this group had also invested more than $1,000,000 in David Alvin's project. People get killed for a lot less than $1,000,000.

Attorney General

Once you realize how the paperwork works in real estate and you sit down with motivated individuals, it becomes very easy to take advantage of them. This could, however, lead to jail time. I have had people sign paperwork and say, "Ross, I really have no clue what I just signed." Because I am aboveboard and believe in karma, I re-explain everything and go through each line in the contract with them.

Some people in the business, however, purposely keep homeowners confused in order to steal their house. Just recently, an individual I know was rightfully reported to the attorney general. He disguised the purchase of a property as a loan. The homeowners had no idea they had sold their home. The perpetrator would have evicted the family and made a handsome profit if someone had not stepped in.

The person who intervened in this case was a friend of mine. He got a phone call from a couple wanting to sell their home to avoid foreclosure. He sat down with the homeowners and listened to their problems. There were some medical issues that had come up, and the homeowners had fallen 30 days behind and told him they were being "evicted." My friend was confused because a mortgage company cannot evict you; they must foreclose on you. After reviewing their paperwork, he quickly realized the homeowners were actually not homeowners, since they had sold their home eight months prior. After pulling up the homeowner's deed, his suspicion was confirmed.

When he explained to the homeowners that they had not received a loan, but had actually sold their home, they became hysterical. There was quite a bit of equity in the house and they did not want to be left with nothing. The wife started crying, and the husband just sat there, quite embarrassed he had made such a tragic mistake.

How did this happen? Months earlier, when the homeowners needed to borrow money to take care of medical expenses, they had an individual randomly knock on their door and offer them the funds they needed. They were so relieved they signed whatever was put in front of them. Unbeknownst to them, they signed the deed to their home. The shady individual then brought the deed to a notary, and without the homeowners present, had the deed notarized, and thus knowingly recorded fraudulent paperwork.

This can happen to anyone. An investor and I purchased a house from a guy who forged his grandma's signature and recorded the deed. He took the $50,000 we had put down and ran.

I'm telling you all this for a couple of reasons. One: Be careful all around. There is a lot of money in real estate, and we all know what people will do for money. Two: Don't join the dark side of shyster investors. Every get-rich-quick investor I have run into eventually falls into some very hard financial or legal times. If you dream of retiring rich off real estate and sitting in a beach chair, be patient with the building of your real estate business. Stay away from the get-rich-quick deals and look for the stay-rich-long deal.

Attorneys Can Get You Arrested
The Renter From Hell

I got a phone call one day from a gentleman about to lose his house to foreclosure. He lived out of town and agreed to sell me his home for $50,000. It needed about $20,000 in work and was worth about $150,000. The home currently had a renter in the property. The best thing about this house was that homes in the area that were in move-in condition were selling within about 10 days. (And it was not until I started to deal with his tenant that I realized why he sold the home so cheap.) Because of the current good market, I decided to get a six-month loan. This meant I would have to have the money paid off in full in six months, or I would face foreclosure.

I started to rehab the outside of the home, and at first, all was well. But the tenant, although he kept telling us he would be out in a couple of days, would not leave. I consulted with my attorney to review my options, and was advised that because of the type of deed that was transferred, the tenant had no legal claim to the house and we could legally remove all objects. We made the tenant aware of this and gave him a week to be out. A week went by and he was still in the home. Prior to entering the property, I called my lawyer and asked, "Are you sure I can enter the home?" My attorney assured me it was my legal right. This turned out to be very bad advice. (Don't believe everything your attorney tells you.)

Acting on this advice, I kicked the door down and changed the locks. The neighbors had been complaining about some junk cars on the front lawn, and since my attorney had told me legally they were mine, I had them towed.

Fast forward to my first time in eviction court: I explained my situation to the judge, thinking it was an open-and-shut case. Well, the judge did not like the fact that I went into the house. She told me I had better read a book on real estate (how ironic!) or my little house-flipping business could lead to a lawsuit.

After the trial I asked the tenant, "What is it going to take to get you to just move out?" He claimed there was an antique sterling silver tea set he'd won on *The Price Is Right* that had been stored in one of the old junk cars. (I didn't know *The Price Is Right* gave away antiques!) He said I had better give him a tea set or $14,000.

I told him, "Sorry, the car has been crushed, and it was your fault for keeping anything of value in a junk car."

Well, he didn't like that very much. About two weeks later I received a letter from his lawyer stating there had also been an urn in the car, and since it was stolen, I would be charged for stealing a body and could face five years in jail. *What?* I had to ask myself, "How did we get here?"

Believe it or not, it gets better. I was three months into the six months of my hard money loan and this deal was not going well. I decided to cut my losses and sell the home to a fellow investor for what I had in it. I let him know I was having difficulties getting a renter out. This experienced investor had a good understanding of the situation and had been through similar situations many times. I sold him the home for what I owed. The investor took the individual to court a few weeks after purchasing the home from me. During the hearing the tenant faked a seizer! This award winning act bought the tenant another month in the home. This was his last pathetic attempt at staying in the home for free. The tenant finally realized he was out of options. The next time he was taken to court he was finally evicted out of the home. A week after this court ruling, I received a call from the fire marshal. The renter burned the house down! Thank God, I had already sold it, or I would have been in foreclosure. Luckily, nothing ever came from any of the other allegations against me.

Looking back: *If you are really trying to make it big in real estate, you will constantly be looking for the big players. You start to get into a realm to which you might not be accustomed. There is a ton of money in real estate and the greed increases with the dollar amounts. The laws are not black and white, and your morals will be tested. Remember this: There is enough to go around and givers gain. You will attract the vibes you put out. Get into this business with the right state of mind and use your power for good.*

Research: *Learn what hard money is.*

Homework: *Find some hard money sources and review their lending guild lines.*

Chapter 14—Role Models

"Hang with dogs with fleas, get fleas; hang with dogs with money, get money."

"What five people do you hang out with most? Average out their incomes. There is more than a good chance your income is within 10 percent of the average."

Let's Add Some Fuel
August 8, 2007

About 18 months ago, I met a young land developer. The 28-year-old had successfully bought and developed many parcels of land. This is the only individual I have run across that I wanted to be when I was his age. Until I met Adam, all the other investors I met, especially land developers, were in their forties.

For the past 18 months I have been doing my best to stay in touch with Adam, hoping to get an opportunity to work with him. About 75 percent of the time he would not return my phone calls or e-mails. Why should he? I had nothing to offer him. However, I knew I could not let this connection slip. Staying in touch with him eventually earned me an even $100,000 on one deal. This is how it happened: About 45 days prior I spoke with Adam, and as always, I asked him if he had anything I could help him with.

To my surprise, he replied: "Ya know what, Ross, I do. Help me liquidate this land I own."

To make a long story short, I leveraged my Rolodex and found a buyer to purchase the land for $1,500,000 within two weeks. Finding this buyer put me in Adam's good graces. Now I would be able to observe how he did business and get in on the ground floor on a couple of his investments. I want to learn first-hand how he was making his money.

After helping Adam sell his land, I have built value in our business relationship and given Adam a reason to keep in touch. These next few paragraphs are included in the book to help keep you persist in your efforts to reach your goal of success in real estate. As we all know, if you're not persistent, you're nothing.

If you're older than Adam, I hope you use this information to say to yourself, "That guy is younger than me; if he can do it, I can do it."

If you're young, I just want you to understand the dream is possible. Everyone who knows Adam knows he is wealthy. However, the several times I met him he was driving a 2001 Jimmy. Unfortunately, in this society I can't help but look at someone's car and judge his or her wealth status. About two weeks ago, I went to Adam's house to put together the contracts for our land deal. When I pulled up to the driveway, any doubts I might have had about his wealth evaporated. Adam lives in a 7,500 square-foot house on the water and is in the process of building an amazing pool in his 1.5-acre back yard. I asked him about his car, and he replied, "I don't like buying depreciating assets."

Meeting young individuals far more successful than me helps fuel my motivation for great success. To encourage you even more, let me briefly summarize some of this 28-year-old's recent investments. He purchased a piece of undervalued land for under $600,000 and sold it three months later for $1,800,000. He is currently building a 400-

unit condo complex in another state, and owns hundreds of acres from Florida to Maryland.

The next question I can't help but ask myself is where is he finding these investments? Every time I brought him what seemed like a great deal he would quickly kill my enthusiasm by telling me what he had paid for similar land. While we were looking over some of his projects, I decided to be bold and just ask: "Where do you find most of your land deals?" This is a question most people will not answer; however, after a couple of rum and cokes, he told me it was from the timber companies. He is on a list and the timber company sends him upcoming properties for sale. He showed me the package he gets in the mail and told me to keep it quiet. He just sits back and waits for the mail, puts his values on the properties, and makes an offer. I noticed a phone number on the package he showed me. Guess who is now on the list?

Looking back: *When you find someone young connected and successful in town do not let go. It took me years to become a close associate with this individual. I had to keep on giving and giving and giving. Now we communicate on almost a daily basis and work on projects together. We will continue to make a ton of money together probably for decades. In this section I briefly spoke about developing land; however, I want to make it clear that land development is very complex. Do not even think about land development for the first several years of your investing career. Developing large parcels of land has a political aspect to it that is very different from buying and selling homes.*

Chapter 15—Insanity

"If one person can do something, anyone can learn to do it." —NLP, the new technology of achievement

The Need for Private Funds

What's the difference between the investor who's running around 60 hours a week, and doesn't "feel" like he or she has any money but is worth a lot on paper—and the investor who has employees managing his properties, drives a very nice paid-for car, and feels rich, so he or she is always attracting opportunity? Many times the answer to that question is simply access to private funds. My goal has always been to get as many good deals as possible. "If the deal is good, money will never be an issue." That is a quote I used for years. Never say never.

Well, money is becoming an issue. Currently it has become much more difficult to obtain financing for properties all across the United States. We are in what the headlines call "the mortgage crisis." A ridiculously large amount of loans are in default, and it is affecting investors in all areas. From real estate to the stock market, America has felt a sharp punch in the financial stomach.

If you want to be successful in real estate, private funds are an absolute must. From the first day you find your "why" and decide to become a real estate investor, you need to keep your ears and eyes open for a private lender. Private lenders can be anyone—relatives, friends, business associates, anyone with at least $10,000 can be a private investor. Having access to private money is essential if you want to take your investing to the next level. If you have just decided to become a real estate investor, it will be an uphill battle to get people to trust you with their money. However, you need to make it a vital part of your business to reach success. I strongly advocate buying a course on how to find and win over private lenders.

Yes, another course, and this one—just like the two prior course suggestions—is a must. If you miss out on one deal because you can't get it funded, that could be a potential loss of tens of thousands of dollars. I'm speaking from experience. I'm not trying to sell you a course. I'm just giving you the advice I wish I had received.

Earlier in this book, I introduced the concept of buying properties *subject to*. One of the best benefits of purchasing properties *subject to the mortgage* is the minimal amount you need to invest up front. Make that minimal $5,000 to $15,000 investment ten times in a month, and it starts to get very expensive. You are able to leverage $100,000 into 10 properties with huge amounts of equity, but the bottom line is that if you spend $100,000 you feel broke, and if you feel broke you *are* broke. Instead of spending the $100,000 yourself, use private lenders. Now, you have a large amount of equity with all your money still in the bank.

Let's take this example one advantageous step further; borrow an extra $2,500 to $5,000 per property, and buy 10 properties. You just put $50,000 in your pocket. You don't feel broke anymore. You have the funds available to expand your business, hire employees, and increase your marketing budget. As you're using OPM, your properties are selling while you're buying, and you are putting $100,000 a month in your pocket. It's very possible with private funds.

Something to look forward to on your search for private funds is the people you meet on the way. You will obviously be searching for people with money. These are successful people; successful people typically have good resources and know other successful people—thus providing you with access to more resources, more ways to leverage other people's money, and resources to help in your goal of becoming modern-day royalty.

A Huge Accomplishment
November 5, 2007

In August 2004, I attended *Real Seminar Secrets of Local Real Estate Investors*. Today I have been asked to speak at the exact same type of venue. It seems like just yesterday I was attending my first real estate seminar where I met my mentor, John. I am grateful to him for teaching me the skills that will keep my family wealthy forever—and in return, I helped him make a lot of money. I helped him acquire more than 150 homes, apartment complexes, land, trailer parks, and a golf course. During all of those ventures I made priceless contacts and built an impressive portfolio for myself. At 25, I have been recognized by my community as a real estate "guru."

Phrases Worth Mentioning

There is one phrase that helps me so much in so many ways that I feel it is worth mentioning. It is "Let me ask my partner." No matter if you have a partner or not, if people think you do, it will help in all negotiations. How does this help? Your partner is always the bad guy. Whenever you don't agree, you can strongly take the opinion of the person you're negotiating with, and try your hardest to get your "partner" to agree. I have found this helps work out win-win solutions.

Sometimes people don't want to sign on the dotted line simply because you are making too much money. I often nip that concern in the bud early, explaining that I have to split proceeds with my partner/ partners.

Another advantage is that when something goes very wrong, you have someone to blame. I believe it's a strong character trait to take the blame when something you are a part of goes wrong; however, sooner or later there will be a situation where publicly taking the blame in a negotiation might amortize the deal—and who better than your "partner"?

Am I Insane?

The file *My Book* has been saved on my desktop for more than seven years now. Every morning when I turn on my computer, I see the file *My Book* on my computer desktop and I kind of laugh. Doesn't it seem a little insane that I started writing a book on how to become wealthy when I was dead broke? Who was I to start writing a book about making millions in real estate at a time when I had less than $2,000 in the bank? What was I thinking, spending hours of my time organizing a book on how to become wealthy when I was actually broke?

What I was thinking was: "I am going to be a modern-day king." Ask yourself a question: Do you think it was a coincidence I have been so successful, or did I just get lucky? I'd rather be lucky than good; however, my success has had nothing to do with luck or a coincidence. Every day when I made that decision to keep pushing toward my goals, reviewing my reasons why, and pouring all my time into organizing a system, did it ever dawn on me that maybe I can't do this? The honest answer to that is yes. There were many moments when I thought I could not reach my goals. However I just continued to complete small proactive actions each day. Had I given up, I would have never become a successful real estate investor, I would not be a published author, and I would have never had the amazing opportunity to help countless people reach their definition of financial success.

This time four years ago I was a zero with an idea. In four years I have turned a broke kid into a financially free real estate guru. Every time I review my book it reminds me how far I have come. And I know you can do the same. Your daily efforts will build on each other just like compounded interest, the most powerful force in the universe. In this business, when you first start you will feel like you are not making any progress. My advice to you is to come up with a way to look back. When you're four years old, you're growing very fast, but because you look in the mirror every day, you don't notice it. However, if every six months you measure yourself and put a line on the wall a year from now, you will see how far you have come. You can look back in many different ways. The way I look back is through writing and reviewing this book.

Write your own book. Come up with a title along the lines of your financial goal. If your goal is to make $2 million this year, call the book *How to Make $2 Million in a Year.* This is a more powerful exercise than you might realize. It will bring into your mind the reality that you are already successful. Write the book as if you already know you are going to be successful, because you are. Everyone has certain difficulties in their life; in your book, define your difficulties and write about how to overcome them. Give the readers of your book advice on how to stay motivated, and include your personal stories of success. Most importantly, find people with whom you can share your book. Before you know it, you will be writing page 100 and have a very impressive real estate portfolio.

Create your title right now, and start on chapter one.

Title: *How to* _____ *in* _____ *months*
Chapter 1: Why I decided to invest in real estate
Chapter 2: How I plan to overcome

The Mindset

Every successful person is a firm believer in training one's own mind for success. I recommended you writing a book on how to reach your goals. Sharing with you what my writing exercise did for me and what it had done for other successful entrepreneurs should motivate you. The power behind this exercise is to firmly plant success in your mind. Giving yourself a feeling of achievement brings your goals into reality.

The truth of the matter is, we all want success—but to dig even deeper than that, we all want the *feeling* of success. The beautiful thing is that you can feel success today. Perhaps the only instant gratification you obtain in real estate is the success state of mind. Do it right now. Put down the book, think about your goals, and visualize where you want to be. Visualize everyone being proud of you, people who once rolled their eyes at your lofty dreams now asking for advice. Boyfriends or girlfriends wishing they were still with you.

You are going to need a big tax write-off, so visualize yourself walking up to the BMW dealership ready to write a check for whatever car you want. Driving away from the dealership in your M5 and quickly going to a charity to help the less fortunate. Whatever feeling you are after, just feel it.

Chances are you just skimmed over the preceding paragraph and decided to visualize your dreams later. Whether you did that or not is actually a good indicator of *when* you will live your dream. Your goal may be to finish this book fast, but if your goal is to be successful, please, just take the five minutes and have fun visualizing your goals. Make sure to use each one of your senses.

To practice what I preach, I am going to do this with you. I picture myself being interviewed about my book and here's what I see: Donald Trump has read my book, and being the smart businessman he is, saw a niche in the real estate market of younger investors. Since he does not yet have the money to travel back in time, he decides to team up with me. We negotiate for a couple of weeks about profit share, and after coming to a win-win agreement, contracts are signed. He sets up interviews and I'm off. I just got off a plane five hours ago and my body is a little tired, but the four coffees I nervously consumed are keeping my mind awake. My first interview is on an investing radio show on satellite radio. While I'm waiting, I see a couple of small-time celebrities, give them a copy of my book, and in a few minutes I hear "Mr. Hamilton, you're on in five." I walk into the studio, which smells a little of cigarettes because the host just finished smoking outside during a break. I sit on a hard stool and briefly get introduced to the host. I see a girl put her hand up and go "5-4-3-2-1, you're on." The host instantly talks about my book—the very part you are reading right now. People call in, and I field all the questions perfectly. I put in a quick pitch for connectedinvestors.com and some of Donald Trump's businesses, and I'm done. Overnight, book sales soar, and I help countless people realize their dreams of success.

It takes about three minutes to visualize, and boy is it fun! To fully answer any questions on why any of this is important, I need some extra help from an expert. I highly recommend you buy the book *Think and Grow Rich* by Napoleon Hill. Like so many other authors have done, I could write my own version of the book, but I would be doing you a horrible injustice. Napoleon Hill devoted over 25 years of his life to writing the philosophy of success. I just turned 25. If you have already read what I consider to be the Bible of success, *Think and Grow Rich*, read it again. You want to study Mr. Hill's book. I keep it on my desk and read it every day.

Since we all like instant gratification, I also suggest you go to YouTube and type in "Napoleon Hill." One of the search results will show up in black-and-white video entitled "Napoleon Hill speaking about his meeting with Andrew Carnegie." Watch it. I watch it every day before I check my e-mail.

Why is Hill's book so good? It is complete. He has, for example, an entire chapter devoted to channeling your sex drive into a success drive.

We all know a guy, or you might just be the kind of guy, whose sole goal is to attract the opposite sex. He delights in the chase for women that most people are scared to talk to. All he ever talks about is ways to "get" her. His mind never stops coming up with the most elaborate, off-the-wall plans to do so. He forms friendships and alliances with people for the sole reason of getting closer to the women he wants. He spends an insane amount of money on things to bring him closer to his goal. He asks everyone for advice. He visualizes what it would be like to be with her every day. He has been turned down 100 times but it does not faze him. If he had an opportunity, he would skip any important activity to capitalize. And guess what? More often than not, despite the odds, he gets the girl. Think how powerful that same motivation would be if he applied it toward success.

The first time I picked up *Think and Grow Rich*, I skimmed through the chapters and noticed one called "The Mystery of Sex Transmutation." I read the first couple of pages and knew the author had a thorough understanding of the philosophy of success.

Put down my book and read his book. There is a chapter on organized planning and—where he leaves off is the point where my book comes in. To be specific, many people read *Think and Grow Rich* and get all hyped up, but when it comes to the organized planning part, they don't quite know what route to take. After completing my book, you will know how to organize your plans for success.

As you read my book, you are riding in the passenger seat of a young millionaire's car on the way to success. I did not jump in the car, drive to success, and then years later try to reminisce on how I did what I did. You are on the most important journey of my life with me, and I sincerely appreciate the company.

Looking back: *It was not until I changed my way of thinking about life that success truly set in. When you are a very young child you believe anything is possible; then somewhere along the way you stop believing. Start believing and start acting.*

We all get into real estate for the same reason. We want to make a bunch of money so we can have a bunch of fun. There is no reason you can't enjoy the ride.

Research: *Find and study the book, Think and Grow Rich; by Napoleon Hill*

Homework: *Start to write your own book on how to become a real estate millionaire!*

Chapter 16—My Best Practical Tips

"Start with the end in mind."—Stephen R. Covey, *The 7 Habits of Highly Effective People.*

Lists Are Power
December 18, 2007

"It's not what you know, it's who you know."

"He is successful because his dad is…"

"The only reason she made it is because she knew…"

We have all heard envious individuals make excuses explaining why someone is successful and they are not, and it is typically because the other person "knew someone." We have probably all made that excuse, I know I have. It's true, a reason Donald Trump rose to royalty so fast is because of his dad and his dad's connections. That was step one, and in step two he leveraged his contacts and executed a plan to become a real estate king. Today we have his daughter, and although looks can certainly help you, without her father's connections she would likely just be a mildly successful real estate agent.

Your list is your "who you know." It's "someone" you go to, to get answers to your questions.

"Do you know anyone who can…?"

"What would you do if…"

"Do you know someone who has a bunch of money?"

"Do you know someone who needs to sell their property?"

"Do you know someone who has a good investment?"

"Who can I trust?"

"Do you know someone who can give me advice on...?"

"How do you...."

"How can I save money on...?"

"Do I need to spend money on...?"

"How can I get rich?"

Donald Trump's daughter can get any of these questions answered in one minute. Developing New York City does not seem hard if you have someone to go to for all the answers. If you're a person who can easily get the knowledge necessary to produce the correct answers, guess what? You're a pro. You don't have to clog your brain with all the answers. You just have to build a list of the right people who have the answers. You have to build your life list of advisors.

Why would someone waste their time giving you the answers? Probably not just because of your dazzling smile. It has to be a win-win relationship. You have to be able to fill in a blank for them. So you must become an expert in one thing. This is important. You need to be the go-to guy/gal for (fill in the blank) and let everyone know you are—not only everyone you know, but people you don't even know. People keep in touch with me because I specialize in working out amazing deals in residential real estate and because I have access to hard money. If your just starting out I know what you are thinking.

"What do I have to offer if I don't even know what I am doing yet?"

When you first start out, the only thing you have to sell is your hustle. Who do you want to be? Find the closest model of that ideal person and do not let go. Help that person accomplish his or her goals. Eventually, you will catch on to what they are doing, and gradually people will recognize your knowledge.

Now that there's no doubt that you need to know people, let's deal with the obvious question: "How do I build my list, and who should I put on it?" Since you're reading this book, your goal is to be a successful real estate investor. You need to speak to as many real estate professionals as possible. More important than speaking with these professionals, you need to brand into their mind that you're an investor. This will take more than one conversation. You must stay in touch indefinitely, don't worry this process can easily be automated with e-mail marketing.

Let's say you meet Rob, a real estate agent, and have a nice little conversation. You both agree you should do business together, and then you exchange cards and go your separate ways. You might send each other an e-mail or two, but inevitably, your relationship fades.

Six months down the line Rob has something for you, but it has been so long he's forgotten about you. You just lost a deal.

How can you keep in touch with everyone you meet indefinitely? Set up an e-mail marketing campaign and put every person you meet on the list. Set it up so that every 60 days people on the list will automatically get an e-mail from you reminding them what you do and asking them how you can help them. I have four different types of lists I put people on:

1. Realtors/investors

2. Mortgage brokers

3. Rent-to-own clients

4. Just saying hello

My Realtor/investor list gets an e-mail once every 60 days saying hello, asking them how business is, telling them what I do, and asking if there is any way I can help them. I have sold several houses to people on this list.

My mortgage broker list gets a similar e-mail once every 60 days, but additionally, I offer them hard money and explain that I can help clients pull together funds if they are facing foreclosure. Mortgage brokers have brought me more business than Realtors.

The rent-to-own list is a record of people who want to lease with the option to buy. They get an e-mail explaining the process and asking how much they can afford a month. When I have a house I need to fill, I have prepared ahead of time.

The just saying hello list consists of those people with whom you just want to keep in touch. The e-mails are very short, asking how business is and telling them I have been very busy buying and selling real estate. This list consists of doctors, lawyers, successful people, friends—people I randomly met.

Once you implement this, you will be able to stay in contact with everyone you meet, remind them what you do, and most importantly ask them if they need help with anything. It is important not to send out too many e-mails; one every 60 days will do the job and avoid annoying people.

Typically, after someone has referred or tried to refer me business, I get their mailing address and date of birth, and make sure they receive a thank you card, Christmas card, and birthday card every year.

If I ever need help with something and can't find the answer, I ask my list. Typically, more than a few people respond with advice.

You will now do business with Rob for the rest of your life. You became his go-to-guy for....

Real estate is a moving puzzle of issues that need decisions. You are looking for people who can give you the correct answers or direction. If you want to rise to royalty through real estate you must be able to get any question answered accurately and quickly. If you do not yet have a real estate area of expertise, become an expert at being able to leverage other people's knowledge. While you are speaking with successful individuals you will find an aspect of real estate you enjoy. Once you find that aspect, really focus on it so you can become the expert in a specific topic.

Secret Service
January 1, 2008

Last week an investor I met at my local REIA took me out to lunch to pick my brain. This is quite a compliment, considering he was twice my age. The cool thing about real estate is, no matter who you talk to, everyone wants to do it because everyone knows you can make a lot of money at it. While we were eating our appetizer, I asked him about his past employment. The gentleman I was sitting down with turned out to be a retired secret service agent! I asked him about his views on the White House, and he asked me for advice on some of his projects. Just a few minutes into the meeting, this secret service agent said, "Ross, you're my hero."

Flattered, I graciously thanked him for his comment and told him he was the hero for serving the country for so many years. We continued to brainstorm on real estate investing strategies, and I asked him one of my favorite questions: "How can I help you make more money?"

This question will put a smile on anyone's face and cut to the chase of what they want out of you. At the end of the meeting we agreed to do business together, and he decided to help me fund some of my projects. I made sure to put him on my list!

Looking back: My entire business model is based on building lists of end buyers prior to introducing a product. This shift in business practice will provide you with more profits then you ever thought possible. When I mentor real estate investors, I teach them to build huge lists of end users prior to purchasing their first home. Starting with your exit strategy is how you should go into any situation.

Research: Learn what an e-mail drip campaign is. Learn what a squeeze page is.

Homework: Search around the net for an e-mail marketing campaign.

Chapter 17—A Punk Kid
with a Ton of Money

"Fake it 'til you make it." Meaning:
"Act the way you want to be
and soon you will become the way you act."

Real Thoughts
February 28, 2009

Currently I am on a plane flying to Vegas to see a few shows and just enjoy life. That's right! I went from a punk kid wanting to flip a house or two to a self-proclaimed punk real estate "guru." You saw the transformation, first hand. I am now 26 years old, about to be married to an amazing woman who has been with me since I had $36 in my account. Even after the real estate crash (which did not hurt me) I still have a real estate net worth of well over $1 million.

The thoughts I held onto every day in my mind have come out of the abstract and into a reality that I can now live. I have no boss, do not wake up to an alarm clock, and take all the vacations I want.

Over the past several months I have spent over two weeks in Central America, partied at the Playboy Mansion, and went snowboarding on several weekend trips. Once I get back from Vegas, I am heading back to Central America to buy some real estate and hang out with friends. My fiancée and I already have long trips set for some of the most beautiful locations all around the world. Life does not suck, and I owe it all to real estate investing. The first words of this book were written when I was just 18 years old. At 18 I identified my definite purpose, my reason why. This reason kept my dreams clear in my mind and motivation pumping through my veins. Identify your reason why, complete the tasks I assigned you, and work toward your dreams.

Real estate investing got me to the Playboy mansion!

That is right my friends, due to my success in real estate I received an invite to a benefit being held at the famous Playboy mansion, a place I never thought I would go. This brings me back to the quote I identified with back in January of 2005:

"In this country, you gotta make the money first. Then when you get the money, you get the power. Then when you get the power, then you get the woman."
- Al Pacino, in Scarface

There was a lot of money raised for a great charity and my fiancé and I had the time of our lives.

A big part of teaching real estate investing is motivation. Prior to publishing this book, our research indicated that 87% of individuals who picked up this book would be male. We knew the title would catch your attention. If you are someone who is not motivated by getting invites to places like the Playboy mansion, know that the title was mainly used as an attention catcher. Guess what? It worked.

I want you to get out a pen and just write down the three important success tips below.

1)   As much as possible, review why you want to be successful & your investing goals. By now you should already have this written down. If you don't have your goals written down, you will probably not be successful.

2)   Find people who have accomplished what you dream of and latch on to them like a parasite. These individuals will be vital to your success.

3)   BE PERSISTENT. No matter your education, status, financial stability, if you are nothing but persistent, success will come.

A Look Back at the Real Estate Crash

The country was in shambles. Foreclosures on the rise, the big guys liquidating, banks giving away houses, government bail-outs, bankruptcies, people burning down their own homes, new laws, the stock market falling, people losing their retirement, no one can get loans, etc…

How did I manage to make more money while the sky was falling then when the market was stable? Most of my detailed secrets are being revealed in my next book, but I will give you a quick overview.

I did not over-leverage myself when things were good.

I did not buy depreciating assets such as a boat, (All my friends have boats) To this day I still have a paid off car)

I did not pull all the money out of my equity lines,

I did not pretend to have money.

I did not think I knew it all and give up on further education

Most importantly, I kept my overhead low.

Once things fell everyone decides to do is to "trim the fat", cutting unnecessary monthly expenses. I never had any "fat"! Everyone has their vices, and I am no exception. I have always enjoyed traveling, but I never brought on any luxury overhead expense.

The first words of this book were written while I was living as a broke college kid. I am finishing this book from a beautiful Nicaraguan villa, looking over some of the most beautiful landscape the world has to offer. The only thing I am worried about getting is too much sun. Everyone else in the United States is worried about paying their mortgage payment—a payment they could probably not afford. But they were trying to "keep up with the Joneses." And now they were probably watching CNN on their state-of-the-art televisions hoping the new administration would bail them out.

What are some of the main reasons I have been consistently doubling my income every year? I was very lucky. (I would rather be lucky than smart!) The market I decided to invest in did not get hit half as hard as the rest of the country. However, many people around me still slowly sunk. The main reason so many people in my area sunk is because they stopped educating themselves. Once you stop learning you stop earning.

Right now is a great time to get into real estate. In fact, it is the best time in many decades. Just do it. The technology is better than ever, information is everywhere, and no problem should stop you. If it does not happen for you, it is because you do not have a strong enough reason why.

Now that you are done reading this book, I would like you to complete this exercise: Journey into the future, three years from now. Close your eyes and visualize the person you want to be. Feel the successes you have had over the last three years. Really focus on how this makes you feel.

Do you have a radiating feeling come over your chest?
Do you feel your face slightly smiling?
Can you almost feel your eyes tear up?

Once you open your eyes ask yourself this question: What one small thing can I do right now that will bring me closer to that feeling?

Complete this exercise every day and you *will* reach your goals. The feeling you had during this simple yet amazingly effective exercise is your intangible - is your reason why. Remember what I wrote in the second chapter: "Before you read any further, I want to make it very clear that if you wish to multiply your chances for success, you need a reason *why* you want to succeed. This will be the fuel to keep your inner desire burning."

"Divine power, I ask not for more riches but more wisdom to make use of the riches you gave me at birth consisting of the power to control and direct my mind to whatever ends I desire."—Napoleon Hill

The only resource you will need is ConnectedInvestors. com. This is an invitation-only resource. You must use code "ross" to get access.
Within this site you can find:

1.   Education/courses

2.   Mentors

3.   Investors

4.   Countless supply of resources

5.   Local investment groups

6.   Investment opportunities

7.   Other young motivated individuals on their rise to royalty

Bonus Information:
Real estate automation
case studies

$28,000.00 in my pocket
In two weeks
Only working a total of 5 hours
While on vacation.

The ultimate goal for real estate investors is to figure out a way to make a ton of money without working a ton of hours.

Recently I set out half way across the world to answer one question:

Can one amass a huge fortune in Real Estate by working only 2 hours a week?

I am here to tell you – I am living proof that the answer to this question is

Yes, you can!

However, you must have certain automated systems in place in order to attain it.

First, you must identify what it is you are trying to automate. Ultimately, Real Estate is a 'people business' and a major part of being a successful investor is managing people. With systems in place, though, you can remove yourself from the management process and still make a bunch of money.

THE ENVIRONMENT THE STUDY TOOK PLACE IN

Now, I enjoy my work – or, rather, that's the excuse I give myself for working 60 hours a week – so in order to properly conduct my Real Estate Automation Study it was necessary for me to escape work and the rest of my familiar civilization. I had to go to a place where there was no practical way I could jump on the 'net or a phone, even if I wanted to. I have been so obsessed with working that I made certain I couldn't even drive somewhere nearby to jump on the 'net to so much as check my e-mail. This was an extreme study! I had to cut the communication cord cold turkey and, I don't mind saying, it was difficult. I cursed out loud, punched stuff, and was very irritable. I literally went through technology withdrawal. But once the shock wore off, the world had a new light. I was able to actually stop for a siesta in the middle of the day! I jumped in on a soccer game! And, I was able to spend some quality time with my family – without having my trusty computer on my lap.

There are several factors which qualify this as a no B.S. study, during which I pulled in over $28,000.00. in 20 days. Can the new guy, just starting out – simply put up a site and jump on the 'net for 2 hours a week, and easily make $28,000, slim chance. I have dedicated myself to building my systems for years. For a new investor, or someone who has been investing in real estate the non systemized hard way, this study will illustrate what you are working toward, the direction into which you can take your life and your business. The Real Estate success stories you hear about on TV do happen.

Still, we don't sell 'Success Pills' that will dehydrate you in the name of immediate results and leave you worse off down the line. What we are offering you is support, a guide to shaping your whole lifestyle in a way which favors a lasting success. Certainly, I'm not suggesting it will take you years to reach your goals, but, come on people! Don't get caught-up in those faulty success headlines! You are smarter than that!

The real way success is made is like dealing with a celebrity fitness and diet trainer, only in order to get the results you are looking for, you will be required to get on the real estate treadmill – and eat the healthy food.

IDENTIFY THE ABSTRACT

Before you read any further, I want to make one thing very clear: if you seek to multiply your chances for success, you must first know your reason to want to succeed. Knowing your motivation will fuel your efforts to achieve your goals. Part of this study will explain why you should consider expending a great deal of those efforts into building a Real Estate portfolio; for all of this to work, though, you need to tell Real Estate why it should invest in you.

Real Estate has everything you could ever want or dream of. You could become a celebrity like Donald Trump, or live a wealthy, quiet life with all the time in the world for family and friends. Why is it you want to succeed in Real Estate?   Your answer to this question must provide motivation enough to carry you through some financially and personally trying times.

The following should adequately illustrate what the future may hold for you, and that you should be dedicated and COMPLETELY OBSESSED with building systems.

THE STUDY

> "Can one amass a huge fortune in Real Estate by working only 2 hours a week?"

Keep in mind that prior to conducting this study:

1.　　I had been buying and selling real estate for years; (KNOWLEDGE)

2.　　I had a team of people working for me, including a virtual assistant, a partner, a real estate agent and a mortgage broker;　(NETWORKING)

3.　　I had built a strong list of wholesale buyers and,

4.　　I had already become known as the 'go-to guy' in my town as a result of years of networking.

Before I left, I made sure I had all bills on auto-pay, that I'd executed a power of attorney, and had set up auto-responders.　Then, I threw a dart at a map, which landed squarely in Playa Venal in Central America.　There's my destination!　I stayed at a residence 50 miles away from anything resembling the 'net.　It was absolutely beautiful.

TWO PROPERTIES SOLD WHILE I WAS AWAY...
HOUSE ONE –

Initial contact:　606 Aragona Blvd., Jacksonville, NC. I mailed a number of letters to people at properties I knew to have been in pre-foreclosure.　The people at 606 Aragona received my letter, and contacted my company.

The process:　Their call was sent to an answering service, and then retrieved by my partner, who I trained to put homes under contract; I provided the funds to close, which I leveraged from an equity line.

How I sold it:　Info was blasted out to an investor list I have long been building through involvement in the local

REIA. The house was under contract within 48 hours and sold one week later.

Net proceeds waiting for me back in the US: $8K

HOUSE TWO –

Initial Contact: 17 Onsville Place, Jacksonville, NC. One of the gentlemen who knocks on doors for me (I met him at my local REIA) made contact with a homeowner who was about to lose his home to foreclosure, to gather some information. He entered the homeowner's details into my website, which was then auto e-mailed to me.

The process: I spoke with the homeowner for about 20 minutes on the phone, sent my contracts to my door-knocking friend who then put the home under contract on my behalf. An Agent contact of mine oversaw repairs.

How I sold it: I blasted my wholesale list and included my agent's phone number. While I was sitting on a secluded beach several thousand miles from all of it, the house sold. No, I'm sorry… I have to correct myself: the beach was not 100% secluded; **a group of 5 cows was near by.**

Net Proceeds: from sale: $20K

THREE PROPERTIES IN THE PROCESS OF BUYING...

LEAD NUMBER ONE - (THIS IS A COMPLICATED PLAY… BUT A GREAT ONE!)

Initial Contact: I have auto-mailings that go out to people who own their homes with no mortgage – this is called The Free and Clear Mailing. A call came into our answering service and was routed to my partner, who returned the call.

The Process: After a number of conversations and e-mails, the home was under contract. The seller agreed to Seller Finance the home at zero percent interest with Principal Only payments. Meaning that every month, we pay the seller $1,000.00 and the balance of the loan goes down $1,000.00.

Once the home was under contract, I blasted the details of this property to my Lease/Option list and, the same day, I put the home under contract – I already had someone ready to rent-to-own this home!

Details of sale: This home is selling for $245,000.00. Our buyers are putting down $5,000 toward the purchase price and will rent it for three years prior to purchasing the home (they cannot close on the house for 3 years). Due to the kick-ass financing we were able to negotiate, at the end of those three years, the principal will have been paid down over $36,000.00.

Were I to hold on to this deal for 3 years, I would profit approximately $50,000; however, I plan on assigning my financing to a local investor for $15,000. The $15,000 + the $5,000 down will net me $20,000.00.

Estimated proceeds: $20K-$50K

LEAD NUMBER TWO: From a mailing, a seller called my answering service; my partner retrieved the call and thereafter put the home under contract. I have a private investor, who found me online, putting up the funds to close the deal.

LEAD NUMBER THREE: A lead recently came from a gentleman who found me on the 'net. He put a property under contract, but his funding fell though. The home was going into foreclosure so he was in a hurry to close. I am buying this house subject to the terms of the existing financing. Another private investor, whom I also met on the 'net, is putting up the funds to reinstate, repair, and carry the property.

Actual net proceeds: $28,578.36

R.O.T = Return on Time - 307 min invested = 5.2 hours
Actual Hourly Income: $5384.62

Estimated earnings = $78,000.00
Estimated ROT = $7,800.00 per hour.

Automation tools used:

1)   Website(s)

2)   List building services

3)   Answering service

4)   Auto-motivated seller mailings

5)   Partner

6)   Agent /Mortgage Broker

7)   Students (Individuals we "built the dream in."
Review chapter 7)

8)   Property Management Company

9)   Private lenders

10)   Networking plan

The pieces of your real estate puzzle will come one at a time. Get excited, once you have your pieces of the Real Estate automation puzzle in place, you will be able to enjoy huge profits while traveling the world.

SO WHERE DO MOST OF THE DEALS COME FROM?

The number one source of deals has come from networking. This is true for most super successful investors. Once you have a good system of automatically reminding every Real Estate professional you have ever met of what you can offer, the deals will come to you.

My secondary source is through direct mail, aimed at motivated sellers. All of my mailings are automated, have been professionally tested, and include my website address and my business phone number.

You cannot remove the 'people process' from Real Estate 100%. Your continual learning will always be a major part of your Real Estate success; the best way to learn is by networking with knowledgeable people in your industry.

I have put together a resource to provide you with the tools, processes and networking to systemize your real estate business. Need more on how networking and list-building have been the foundation of my Real Estate business?

It's not what you know, it's who you know.

"He is successful because his dad is…"

"The only reason she made it is because she knew…"

NETWORKING OILS EVERY ASPECT OF YOUR BUSINESS

The richest man is the one with the most powerful friends.

~ Don Altobello, to Vincent, Godfather 3

Empower yourself and the investors you know with the powerful system I have put together for you. Visit www. ConnectedInvestors.com and use promo code 'Ross'

Take action review:

Your personal review
Homework and research review
Enlightenment review

Your personal review:

Remember the questions from the beginning of this book?

1. Do you want to be successful?

2. Are you the type of person who takes action?

3. Do you often follow through with your goals?

4. Will you complete at least 1 homework and research assignment?

Take action now or risk losing you freedom. Read the following paragraph out loud!

I have a burning desire not to be a slave to money. A nine-to-five job with one week of vacation is my definition of jail. Having a roof over my head on how much I can make would drown my spirits. Basing my retirement on someone else's company policy or hoping there will still be social security is a gamble I am not willing to take. Having the government tax me before I get paid and then tax me on everything I buy is unnecessary. Not being able to pass a decent legacy to my children would be childish. Not being able to teach my children how to enjoy life by having their money work for them would be embarrassing, and having my boss ask me, "Ross, do you want Thanksgiving or Christmas off this year?" is out of the question and sounds like a loose form of slavery to me.

Homework and Research review:

WARNING: Although I moved over ten million dollars of real estate in my first few years of investing and have done nothing but live real estate for the last 8 years of my life, most of you will come up with a reason not to follow my advice. To be exact, over 80% of you will not complete one homework or research assignment. This book is an easy read because 90% of the learning will come from your homework and research assignments. If you choose not to take the proactive steps necessary you WILL fail. Failing in real estate means; losing a ton of money, foreclosure, bankruptcy, and all of the issues that go along with having no money. These words have been designed to scare you. This business is no joke. I have never lost money on a real estate investment because I continue to educate myself. Real estate can make or break your life. **The homework and research assignments I have given you are not an option.**

Topics you must research:

1.   Study short sales

2.   Understand what a Lease option is

3.   Start to understand how to improve your credit

4.   Understand the amazing tax benefits of being an investor. A good place to start is reviewing the book: "Loopholes of the Rich" By Diane Kennedy

5.   Learn what hard money is.

6.	Study the book, Think and Grow Rich; by Napoleon Hill

7.	Learn what an e-mail drip campaign is, and what a squeeze page is.

Homework assignments:

1.	Find and attend the closest REIA. (Real Estate Investment Association.) Collect at least 5 business cards

2.	Call each of the five investors you met at your local REIA and ask them if you can take them out to lunch. Once you get the chance to sit down with an investor, simply ask each investor how you can help them make money

3.	Find someone who will let you borrow a real estate course on just about any topic. Not a book, a full course with many training manuals, audio, forms, etc.

4.	Visit ConnectedInvestors.com. Sign up with promo code 'Ross' start reviewing some of the educational resources.

5.	Find some hard money sources.

6.	Search around the net for a system that allows you to collect e-mail address and build follow up campaigns.

7.	Start to write your own book on how to become a real estate millionaire.

Extra credit: Take the class to become a real estate agent. You do not have to activate your license, however you need to study the in's and out's of this business.

3. Enlightenment Review:

Find a few quotes that mean something to you. Write them out and put them somewhere you will see every day.

"To apply myself industriously to whatever business I take in hand, and not divert my mind from my business by any foolish project of growing suddenly rich; for industry and patience are the surest means of plenty."
—Ben Franklin

"Whatever type of business you want to own, work for your competition first. Find out how they operate and get all of their contacts. Start your own business learning from your boss' mistakes." —Don Hamilton

"To know the road ahead, ask someone coming back."
—Chinese proverb

"Divine power, I ask not for more riches but more wisdom to make use of the riches you gave me at birth consisting of the power to control and direct my mind to whatever ends I desire."—Napoleon Hill

"'The more money you have, the more problems you have' is not just a quote by rapper Biggie Smalls."

"Compounded interest is the most powerful force in the universe."—Albert Einstein

"Options—the ability to choose—is real power."—Tim Ferriss, The 4-Hour Work Week

"The big shots are only the little shots that kept shooting."— Christopher Morley, Business Inspiration Quotes

"In this country, you gotta make the money first. Then when you get the money, you get the power. Then when you get the power, then you get the woman." —Al Pacino, in Scareface

"The richest man is the one with the most powerful friends."—Altobello to Vincent, Godfather 3

"The beginning is the most important part of the work." —Plato

"Fake it 'til you make it." Meaning: "Act the way you want to be
and soon you will become the way you act." —Random blog

"Start with the end in mind."—Stephen R. Covey, The 7 Habits of Highly Effective People

"The young do not know enough to be prudent, and therefore, they attempt the impossible—and achieve it, generation after generation."—Pearl S. Buck

"If one person can do something, anyone can learn to do it." —NLP, the new technology of achievement

"If you want to show kitchens get your license; if you want to make money learn how to invest in real estate."—John Long

Quotes from the author:

"The frustration of not knowing how to advantageously invest often comes disguised in the feeling of needing to save money."

"Becoming a millionaire is like trying to lift a million pounds. It's only possible with proper leverage."

"Hang with dogs with fleas, get fleas; hang with dogs with money, get money."

"What five people do you hang out with most? Average out their incomes. There is more than a good chance your income is within 10 percent of the average."

"If the deal is good, money will never be an issue."

"You cannot win a game of Monopoly© without real estate" -Ross Hamilton

"A reputation is like a castle of cards: difficult and time-consuming to build, and one wrong move and it's all gone."

"Do not deal with professionals who have been in any business for fewer than five years."

"If cash is king, then credit is queen, and we all know the queen can have a huge influence on what the king can achieve."

"Going to your first real estate closing is like getting married."

"Someone once told me: 'Luck is when opportunity meets preparation.'"

"Starting off with nothing makes it easy to risk everything."

"You don't build your real estate portfolio to rest on; you use your heightened elevation, locate opportunities and jump to the next level of wealth."

"Real estate knowledge without application is like having no knowledge at all."

Made in the USA
Coppell, TX
27 April 2020

22824620R00074